Praise for *Better Off After College*

"College costs can be blinding. This is THE guide to college finance that every prospective student and parent should read so they can make a better-informed decision as they choose where and when to apply and where to attend."

MICHAEL B. HORN, Coauthor,
Choosing College

"Let's face it, understanding and navigating the world of college financial aid is nearly impossible for most people. *Better Off After College* is the much needed road map for anxious families trying to sort through the nomenclature, technical details, complexities, and myths and misconceptions that are rife in the world of financial aid. There is still a lot to digest, but the authors bring clarity and common sense to one of the most important financial decisions that students and their families will make."

DR. PAUL LEBLANC, President,
Southern New Hampshire University

"An excellent practical guide that demystifies the cost of college and the complex and nuanced financial aid process."

DR. PHILOMENA V. MANTELLA,
President, Grand Valley State University

"Attending college is still one of the very best economic investments an individual can make—but today this decision is higher-stakes than in years past, and requires more analysis. *Better Off After College* is a useful and practical guide for students, parents, and families looking to understand this process."

DR. SEAN GALLAGHER,
Executive Professor of Educational Policy,
Northeastern University

"As any parent who has sent a child to college can attest, financial aid is very complicated. Although there's no single solution that will work for everyone, *Better Off After College* addresses financial aid and broader issues around education finance with practical advice to help families make better decisions about how to choose a college and how to fund that choice."

STEPHEN M. SMITH, Cofounder, Naviance

"As a parent and former provost I understand the many hurdles and pitfalls that come with college finances. This book is a much needed primer for parents and students that will help families work their way through the many aspects of paying for college. In a time when student debt is continuing to grow, this book is more important than ever, and will become a useful reference for everyone working with students and families, from college counselors to admissions staff. I will be giving copies of this book to all of the families in the college bound programs I work with."

DR. TERRI GIVENS, Founder and CEO,
The Center for Higher Education Leadership

Better Off *After College*

Better Off
After College

A Guide To Paying For College
With More Aid And Less Debt

SABRINA MANVILLE and NICK DUCOFF
Founders of Edmit

Table of Contents

Introduction

Higher education is a central part of the American dream—whether you are a high school student or an adult working full-time while earning a degree later in life. It opens opportunities, provides upward mobility and makes us healthier and happier people (yes, the data does show that!).

As parents, we aspire for our children to flourish, and to be better off than we are—and for that, we're willing to make countless sacrifices along the way. It may feel like providing them the opportunity to go to college is the last big gift we can give our children before they leave our homes and become independent. And so, we stretch.

But we've also seen the scary numbers and heard the cautionary tales. College tuition is rising faster than inflation, and student loan debt has passed the trillion-dollar mark. College is likely to cost you tens of thousands of dollars per year, perhaps even hundreds of thousands of dollars all-in. And to pay for it, many students and their parents are taking on large amounts of debt. Student debt isn't just a student problem; it's a family problem.

1

The big question: is it worth it?

We hear this question over and over when talking to students and parents about their college decision. Families are debating where to apply, whether to go to a more expensive school over a more affordable one, or sometimes even whether a student should go to college at all. And they want to know how much student debt is too much.

Like so many complex questions, the answer is that **it depends**.

Study after study shows that college does pay off. College graduates make more than $1,000,000 more in a lifetime than high school graduates, on average—which more than pays for the initial tuition costs.

But no one is average. The cost you pay (including interest payments on large loans), the time in college, the economic climate and career choices after college—all of these factors and others can swing the result from positive to negative. The truth is that college is a great investment **when the decision is made well**. But when it's made without careful consideration, it can saddle you with debt for 20 years or more.

We left our jobs as university leaders to start Edmit because we believe you should not have to become an expert in the field of higher education to make a great decision about where and how to send your student to college. We know families are eager for help and overwhelmed by all the numbers, terms, jargon, and process. We also believe you should feel empowered in this process. Really! Colleges are competing aggressively for students—and they need you as much as you need them.

Although the purpose of this book is to give you the best information and advice about the dollars and cents of college, we know that money isn't everything and that college is more than just career preparation for a higher salary. For us, going to college was a seminal life experience—a part of growing up into the people we've become. Perhaps you feel the same way, and perhaps you have certain hopes and dreams about what college will be for your student.

We're here to tell you that you can give them those experiences, and the gift of higher education, without endangering your financial future.

This book is designed to be your primer for every stage of the process: starting with saving, all the way through deciding where to go and how you're going to pay for it. We've been deep in the world of higher education for many years, and this book represents what we think you should understand at every step, and what we would do if starting the process with our children (which we have, with 529 plans for our little ones!). It is organized chronologically—so you can choose where to begin based on where your student is in the process, though many of the fundamental terms we use throughout the book are defined in Chapter Two.

You'll see that we address 'you' frequently in the book and refer to 'your student'—so, who are you? You may well be a parent—but you could be a family member of someone aspiring to college, an advisor or counselor to one, or even a high school student yourself. We've written the book with parents in mind, but we have written with enough depth to be helpful to those with more experience in this topic as well. We are primarily addressing the "traditional" college student: someone who is of high-school age and will be a first-time freshman.

This is not a book on college admissions. We believe that **what you get out of college** is more important than where you get in.

Please also note that this book is written for informational purposes; you should consult with a financial advisor or other professional to determine what may be best for your individual needs.

The Big Picture

Before we dive into what plans you should be making, we want to define the most important concepts in maximizing your college investment.

COLLEGE STICKER PRICE—AND WHY IT DOESN'T MATTER

When you start to research colleges, you'll see that they represent their costs in many different ways (just one of the many complications of this process!).

Colleges are required to calculate and publish a **cost of attendance** (COA), which approximates what it will cost you to attend a school for one year. Tuition, fees, and room and board are typically the largest categories, but colleges can also estimate costs such as books, supplies, transportation, and personal expenses. Every college estimates its own cost of attendance—you can think of it like an average budget.

The expenses for total cost of attendance can vary quite a bit. For instance, dorm prices in coastal cities can be far higher than what you'd pay for comparable living space in other parts of the country. Total cost of attendance can also be lower if a student lives at home. Usually the college's estimate for COA is an average across all of these potential situations.

We will call this the **published price**, since this is the big number on the college website (it's also sometimes called "list price" or "sticker price"). A college's published price is what a student would have to come up with per year if they paid full price for everything.

All that said, **the published price means very little**. Very few students actually pay it. In fact, a 2018 National Association of College and University Business Officers study found that only 12% of students do!

The price you care about is called the **net price**. This is the amount a student or family pays after deducting grants and scholarships (the "free money" from the college). You might cover this cost from your savings, with money you or your student earn, or by taking out student loans.

You **could** be asked to pay published prices. In fact, there will almost always be colleges that want you to pay the published price. But there will almost certainly also be colleges that won't. Here's why: colleges are looking to cover their costs **and** accept a diverse set of students, including academically stronger students who may have a lot of other options. So they are putting together financial aid packages that they believe will make them appealing to the students they want. It's why everyone pays a different price for college and why "tuition discounts" (in the form of financial aid) are very common. In fact, the price families actually pay for college, after financial aid and scholarships, has been rising more slowly in recent years than the published prices.

HOW TO REDUCE *YOUR* PRICE

Some families might say they're willing to pay whatever it takes to go to that dream school. But presumably you are reading this book because you'd prefer not to pay full price! Here's a preview of the top ways to reduce your cost of college. We'll tell you how to do each of them in the book.

- Maximize your financial aid by finding colleges that are going to be generous with students like yours. Even if you are financially comfortable, there are ways for you to get discounted tuition. You'll need to understand how colleges distribute their financial aid and be strategic about what colleges you apply to. It may mean sacrificing prestige or being open to colleges you haven't considered before.
- Many colleges will consider a "financial aid appeal," or a request for more financial aid once you have your initial offer. If you want to have negotiation as an option, you'll need to apply to certain types of colleges and to have the right mix in your college list.
- Keep your financial aid active and budget wisely. Make sure you understand how your financial aid will be calculated annually and what could cause you to lose it. While in college, keep to a budget and look for ways to reduce expenses.

IS COLLEGE ALWAYS WORTH IT?

Researchers at the Federal Reserve Bank of New York have calculated the average return on investment (ROI) for a bachelor's degree to be around 14%, "easily surpassing the threshold for a sound investment." This ROI was calculated based on the cost of an undergraduate education and the college wage premium—or how much more college graduates can expect to earn compared to high school graduates until the age of retirement at 65.

Although we often hear of students with unmanageable student loan debt, the widening wage disparity has kept the college wage premium at an all-time high. Even in the midst of falling wages in the wake of the Great Recession and sharply rising tuition over the last decade, the value of a college degree hasn't flagged because the wages of those without a degree have been falling even more rapidly. In fact, as those with only a high school degree continue to fall behind, getting a college degree may be more important than ever.

The study showed that college graduates with a bachelor's degree earn an average of 75% more in wages than high school graduates, amounting to more than $1 million over a lifetime. The researchers found that although a third of college graduates find themselves sometimes working jobs that do not require their degree, they still tend to earn more than high school graduates on average. Most settle into college-level jobs by age 30. In general, they are far less likely to become or remain underemployed as well. A different report by the Georgetown University Center on Education and the Workforce, *The College Payoff*, puts the lifetime college wage premium at 84%, adding up to about $2.8 million on average.

The research results are averages, though, which means **your mileage may vary.** The same Federal Reserve study above showed that, for about a quarter of graduates, the investment in college did not pay off. Here's why that can happen.

THE FULL COST OF COLLEGE—AND THE FULL COST OF LOANS

It's obvious that how much you pay for college is a key part of the return on investment. The more you pay, the higher the "return" needs to be in order to make it worthwhile. Loans are a key part of this calculus because you'll be paying interest on your loans, adding to the total cost.

YOUR STUDENT'S MAJOR AND CAREER PATH

The wage premium described above will look different depending on career prospects and job opportunities, which correlate with your major as well as with the college you go to. The highest-paying majors, when looking at lifetime earnings, are STEM, health, and business majors, according to *The Economic Value of College Majors*, a 2014 study from Georgetown's Center on Education and the Workforce. The lowest-paying majors, the same study showed, are in education, human services, and the arts.

But it is not true that every student should major in computer science in order to get a good ROI on college. Recent studies show that liberal arts majors can catch up to STEM majors over time, as their salaries grow more quickly later in their careers and many enter management-level and leadership positions using those "soft" skills. Liberal arts majors have a wider array of options (some high- and some low-paying): consider the difference between a lawyer's salary and that of a social worker or teacher.

In some cases, the college you go to will be more important than your major; studies show that graduates of very selective universities, for example, tend to have higher earnings regardless of major. The location of the college also tends to impact the job opportunities for graduates, giving urban universities an advantage in terms of post-graduation earnings.

GRADUATION RATE AND TIME

No one starts college thinking they won't graduate. But the reality is that many college students take longer than four years to graduate, whether it's because they need more time to complete their credits or because life intervenes and they need to take a break to address family or personal issues. Only 65% of students who start their studies at public four-year universities have completed any degree six years later, according to the National Student Clearinghouse. Many students will never finish.

The financial implications? Six years of college costs more than just two more years of tuition; since your student's career start will be delayed, there are two additional years where they won't be earning a college graduate-level salary.

And if you don't graduate at all it is even more costly. People who have college debt but no college degree are trying to pay off loans without the ability to get higher-paying jobs.

GRADUATE SCHOOL

Some majors and career paths pay off most when paired with a graduate degree.

College is expensive, but so is graduate school—often, even more so. There tends to be less financial aid available and prices have risen more quickly for graduate schools than for undergraduate colleges. Graduate school students have on average 3x the debt of undergraduates.

Although your student may think that graduate school is far in the future and unknown, it's worth considering the possibility that if you do go, you'll need to take on student loans unless you have tens of thousands of dollars available in savings. This means that the smaller your existing loans the better.

HOW TO INCREASE *YOUR* COLLEGE ROI

Your confidence in the following factors can help you decide how much you're willing to stretch financially in order to position yourself for a strong ROI. We'll help you understand the tradeoffs throughout the book, and how to have the right conversations along the way.

- Of course, pay less for college and minimize your loans.
- Ensure your student will feel happy and well-supported by the college in order to graduate, and to graduate on time.
- Find colleges with strong career outcomes, career services, and career opportunities. Make this a central part of your research.
- Consider your student's interests and anticipated major. If they aren't sure or are interested in a less lucrative path, you will want to take on less debt so that you can comfortably pay back loans.

Now, let's set up your plan!

CHAPTER ONE

Pre-High School: Saving

Alongside buying a house and saving for retirement, sending children to college is a major financial goal. Some parents are able to start saving for college early, when their children are in diapers. Others get a later start, often by necessity! Regardless of where you are in the process, you're making major strides by committing to save toward this major milestone.

As we'll discuss, there are lots of ways to pay for college—but first, you'll need to have a sense of the numbers.

Most Americans use a combination of methods to pay for college: personal savings, 529 plans, financial aid, loans, and help from family and friends. In this chapter, we'll share some projections about the rising cost of tuition. Next, we'll discuss whether it's better to save for your retirement or your children's college; and, finally, we'll take you through the many twists and turns of a 529 plan and other savings accounts. The goal is to make you an informed consumer, able to send your student to college in a way that makes it as affordable as possible.

HOW MUCH TO SAVE

What will college tuition cost in the future? You don't have to look far or dig deep into statistics to see headlines about the rising price of college and the fact that college prices have been outpacing inflation throughout the past decade. Although we don't have a crystal ball to give you a precise answer, we can look at historical data to give you a sense of what you should be saving.

How Much the Cost of College Increases Annually

The cost to attend college has been steadily climbing throughout the past 30 years—and will likely continue to climb. Estimates vary as to how much, but data from the College Board's *Trends in College Pricing* show that over the past ten years the average published cost (tuition, fees, room and board) of public universities has gone up on average 2.7% per year and the average private university tuition has increased on average 2.4% per year.

Although occasionally colleges will hold tuition steady or even decrease their tuition from year to year, this rarely happens for more than a couple of years at a time before tuition is increased again.

What Can You Expect to Pay?

Recall, however, that the published price doesn't tell the whole story.

While published prices have been on the rise, net prices have held more steady. A number of trends are putting pressure on colleges to become more affordable for the average student.

Published Cost and Net Prices (Tuition, Fees, Room and Board) in 2018 Dollars

Public Four-Year (In-State)

	'97-'98	'07-'08	'13-'14	'14-'15	'15-'16	'16-'17	'17-'18	'18-'19
Published Cost	$11,730	$16,410	$19,830	$20,020	$20,660	$21,100	$21,400	$21,370
Net Price	$9,170	$11,990	$13,630	$13,740	$14,330	$14,790	$14,910	$14,880

Private Nonprofit Four-Year

	'97-'98	'07-'08	'13-'14	'14-'15	'15-'16	'16-'17	'17-'18	'18-'19
Published Cost	$30,400	$38,700	$44,190	$44,900	$46,330	$47,490	$48,380	$48,510
Net Price	$21,330	$25,880	$25,070	$25,170	$26,000	$26,730	$27,160	$27,290

Source: College Board

It's also important to note that average net prices can also vary widely by family income. The following data is from the U.S. Department of Education:

Net Price Paid at Public Four-Year Institutions, by Income Level (2015-2016)	
$0 to $30,000	$9,510
$30,001 to $48,000	$11,200
$48,001 to $75,000	$15,030
$75,001 to $110,000	$19,240
$110,001 or more	$21,880

Net Price Paid at Private Nonprofit Four-Year Institutions, by Income Level (2015-2016)	
$0 to $30,000	$20,150
$30,001 to $48,000	$20,490
$48,001 to $75,000	$23,290
$75,001 to $110,000	$27,080
$110,001 or more	$34,900

Source: *National Center for Education Statistics*

When considering how much to save, look at the trends and estimate how much college is likely to cost a family like yours when your student is attending. Think about whether you want private universities to be an option, and also start to think about how much you'll be willing to contribute—do you aim to cover the full cost or do you expect your student to take on some of the responsibility by working or taking loans?

Nick, one of this book's co-authors, has decided to save for his children's college with the expectation that college will cost about the same in 2036 as it does now! In his view, there are many trends that could reduce the cost of college in the future even though college costs have risen steadily for the last decade. These trends include, for example, the rise of online education—which can be provided more affordably than in-person education—and political proposals to create "free college" options, which could put pressure on all colleges to reduce their prices. Therefore, he plans to be more conservative in his saving than some financial advisors would recommend.

Saving for College or Saving for Retirement

As parents you have a primary responsibility to make sure you will be in a strong position for retirement before you move on to help your children with education expenses. You don't want to risk becoming a liability for your children by prioritizing their educational expenses over the wellbeing of your retirement nest egg.

Nirav Batavia is a CFA and co-Managing Partner of Forum

Financial Management, a Registered Investment Advisor with 3,600 client households and more than $3.8 billion under management. He asks parents three questions to figure out whether and how much a family should save toward their children's education:

First, is your family currently on track for retirement savings? Very simply, if you are not, you should prioritize your retirement. If you are tracking ahead of your goal, it may make sense to redirect some savings for a few years toward education.

Second, if you are on track with your retirement savings, how much should you contribute to education? This is a personal choice based on how much you want to contribute to your children's college. The answer is really dependent on the target for college savings and how much time you have until your children go to college.

Third, could saving for college through a 529 be a waste if the child doesn't attend college? The short answer: usually not. In the next section, we'll address the ins and outs of a 529 investment account. For now you should know that there are some constraints and penalties if you are forced to withdraw the money for non-educational purposes. A non-qualified withdrawal will be taxed at the parents' ordinary income rate plus a 10% penalty on any growth. However, this penalty rarely ever happens because you can change a beneficiary to be any blood relative. Siblings, cousins, or grandchildren can use those 529 assets tax-free. That same strategy applies if your student finishes college and still has a little money left over in their 529. Batavia advises clients to leave it alone with the plan of changing the beneficiary to the grandchildren down the line, allowing the account to continue to grow tax-free.

HOW TO SAVE FOR COLLEGE

Assuming you've decided to put money aside for your student's college, there are several ways you can do that. Below we'll cover 529 plans, which offer tax advantages and conservative investment options, making it easy to save money for post-secondary education expenses. Importantly, even with a 529 college savings plan, you can still obtain financial aid.

The earlier you start saving, the better—but if you are starting later, it may still be very worthwhile. An investment made when your student is in middle school could benefit from five to seven years of growth to reduce the cost of college. Even for students in high school, parents can consider investing for the last year or two of college, withdrawing after a few years of tax-free growth. 529 savings can also be used for grad school.

Saving with a 529 Plan

Using a 529 plan, account holders can either prepay a beneficiary's tuition, or fund an account that will be invested and can be used for qualified educational expenses at an eligible institution. The IRS designed 529 plans to help families save for college without being penalized by taxes. States, state agencies, and educational institutions each often have their own 529 plans.

Anyone, including parents, grandparents, other family members, and friends, can open an account for an eligible beneficiary. Parents and grandparents can open separate 529 plans for a child at the time of birth. Although it's most common to open a 529 plan for dependents, you can also open a 529 plan for your own educational expenses and name yourself a beneficiary.

WILL SAVING AFFECT MY FINANCIAL AID?

A common concern among parents is that saving too much will impact their financial aid. The simple answer is that saving with a 529 plan should not affect your financial aid that much. If the beneficiary of a 529 plan is a dependent of their parents, the 529 plan is considered a parental asset, not a student asset, and is counted less heavily against you for financial aid purposes (more on this in Chapter Two). For parents who are concerned about financial aid eligibility, a 529 college savings plan is ideal.

529 PREPAID TUITION PLANS VS. 529 COLLEGE SAVINGS PLANS

There are two different types of 529 plans: 529 savings plans and 529 prepaid tuition plans.

A 529 savings plan can be used at any eligible institution and is usually created by a state or state agency. Although states are not required to have a 529 plan, every U.S. state has at least one 529 plan, and some states have multiple 529 plans. In most cases, you don't have to be a resident of a specific state to use its 529 plan. For instance, you can reside in California, invest in Utah's My529 plan, and the beneficiary can use the 529 money for your child to attend college in Arizona.

529 savings plans can be opened directly by the state's plan manager or through financial advisors. The advisor plans provide access to those advisors but may involve higher fees as a result.

An eligible educational institution is any institution that is eligible to receive and distribute federal financial aid—and the vast majority of colleges and universities are. 529 plans are most commonly used at four-year colleges and universities, but can also be used at graduate schools, community colleges, private academies, trade, and vocational schools.

529 savings plans can be used for "qualified educational expenses" which include tuition and fees, room and board, books, course supplies, and equipment such as a laptop. It does not include expenses like health insurance or transportation. Student loans cannot be paid off by a 529 plan either. If you haven't used up your 529 savings at graduation, you won't lose the money and can keep it for graduate school, transfer the account to another beneficiary, or withdraw the money with a tax penalty.

529 prepaid tuition plans allow you to prepay tuition by contributing a certain amount annually. The annual contribution is converted to a "tuition certificate," which can be applied to a year of tuition at a partner school. (Note this only covers tuition—not any of the other qualified expenses listed above.) In many cases, states that offer 529 prepaid tuition plans have strict age, residency, and expiration requirements. State plans are usually limited to specific in-state schools and often impose limits on when the money must be used—usually before the beneficiary reaches age 30, or 30 years after the first tuition certificate is purchased.

THE TAX IMPLICATIONS OF A 529 COLLEGE SAVINGS PLAN

There are no federal tax deductions specific to a 529 plan, but what makes them attractive is that you can accrue investment earnings in the account tax-free, so long as the money is used for a qualified higher education expense.

State tax deductions for 529 contributions vary widely. Some limit deductions to 529 account holders contributing to the state plan, while others offer state tax deductions to individuals contributing to any 529 plan, even if it is in another state. States also have different contribution limits on the tax benefits.

HOW TO FIND THE BEST 529 PLAN FOR YOUR NEEDS
There are many factors to consider when choosing a 529 plan, including the college you will attend, higher education expenses, investment options and performance, financial aid, and tax deductions. Your choice for a 529 plan may be different for each student.

To research your options, decide what type of plan you're looking for. Then see what your state offers—in terms of the plans available as well as the tax incentives. If you aren't sure your in-state option will provide the best benefits, you should compare others. Nirav Batavia advises that "if a family isn't tied to their in-state plan because of the state-tax deduction, they should look for low fees, good diversified investment options, and ease of use."

INVESTMENT OPTIONS FOR YOUR 529 PLAN
Most 529 plans offer a limited variety of investment options to choose from—meaning you can designate the types of investments that will be made with your money. The plan administrator (e.g. the state or institution) always determines the offerings, but you can hire a qualified investment advisor to help you choose the best 529 plan options based on what is available when you decide to open an account.

You might also want to consult with a tax advisor and the plan administrator. Some college savings plans and most prepaid tuition plans use an age-based investment model that allocates towards more aggressive investments when the beneficiary is younger and more conservative investments as the beneficiary reaches college age.

It's important to remember that 529 plans are investment accounts and do involve some risk.

If your student is older, choose a plan without age restrictions that will allow you to maximize your investment in less time. If your student is younger, choose an age-based plan that will maximize your investment as the beneficiary reaches college age.

529 PLAN CONTRIBUTION LIMITS

529 plans have very high contribution limits that are designed to reflect the total cost of undergraduate and graduate education for college savings plans, and of undergraduate education for prepaid tuition plans. The lifetime contribution limits for most 529 plans range from $200,000 to $500,000.

However, unless you're the beneficiary, 529 contributions are considered gifts, and the IRS imposes a gift tax on contributions over a certain amount. This means that you can contribute up to $15,000 per year to each child's 529 before you are taxed, or that you and your spouse can contribute $30,000 total per year ($15,000 each) to each child's 529 before you are taxed. The same gift tax also applies to grandparents, relatives, friends, and anyone else who contributes to a 529 plan.

You also have the option to "superfund" a 529 account by giving a five-year annual gift all at once. The benefit of superfunding the account is that with a higher starting balance, the account will accrue higher earnings. Individuals can donate up to $75,000 (couples can donate $150,000) at one time. However, you cannot give another monetary gift to the beneficiary within this five-year period without accruing taxes.

USING THE MONEY IN A 529 PLAN

A 529 distribution must be used for the beneficiary, and must only be used for qualified higher education expenses. The withdrawal limit is equal to the full cost of attendance of the college your student attends (recall this is estimated by the college), with some adjustments based on other tax credits you are taking or other forms of educational assistance.

If the distribution is spent on ineligible expenses or exceeds the limit, it will be subject to a 10% federal penalty. (You do not pay tax on the full distribution—just on the accrued interest.) The amount is also subject to state income tax.

Other College Savings Options

If you are saving money for your student to use for college, the 529 education savings plan and prepaid tuition plans are not your only option. Coverdell Education Savings Accounts (ESA) and the Uniform Gifts to Minors Act (UGMA) and the Uniform Transfer to Minors Act (UTMA) are other options that parents use to set aside money for their children's education.

UGMA/UTMAs are custodial accounts that transfer ownership to the minor once they become of age, and are not designated for any particular use. If there is serious doubt as to whether your child will attend college, or you want to ensure the money remains in control of the beneficiary, a UGMA/UTMA account may be a better option. Since 529 plans are limited to higher education expenses, you risk paying penalties and federal tax and losing state tax benefits if the beneficiary decides not to attend college and you choose not to transfer the 529 account to an eligible family member. With a UGMA/UTMA, the money can be used for any purpose.

A Coverdell ESA, like a 529 plan, offers investment options for parents planning to save for their child's education. But they are only available for families below a certain income level and have an annual contribution limit.

529 Plans vs. Uniform Gift to Minors Act (UGMA)/Uniform Transfer to Minors Act (UTMA)

	529 Plan	UGMA/UTMA
Control	Remains in control of the account holder indefinitely	Automatically transferred to the minor when they turn 18-24, depending on the state
Use	Must be used for qualified educational expenses	Can be used for any expense
Tax Implications	Not taxed if used for qualified higher education expenses	Earnings above standard deduction are taxable
Financial Aid Implications	Assessed as parental assets on the FAFSA (lower negative impact on aid)	Assessed as student asset on the FAFSA (higher negative impact on aid)

529 Plan vs. Coverdell Education Savings Accounts (ESA)

	529 Plan	Coverdell ESA
Age Restrictions	None	Account can accept contributions until the beneficiary is 18, and the funds must be used by their 30th birthday
Usage	Must be used for qualified educational expenses	Must be used for qualified educational expenses, with a longer list that includes more K12 expenses than a 529 plan
Tax Implications	Dependent on state	Tax-free growth and withdrawals if used for qualified expenses
Income Limits	No income requirements for account holders	$95,000 to $110,000 (single) and $190,000 to $220,000 (joint)
Contribution Limits	529 plans don't have annual contribution limits, though contributions over $15,000 are subject to the gift tax	$2,000 per beneficiary, per year

TAKEAWAYS

- The cost of college is high and could continue to rise—but the net price that parents typically pay for college can be considerably less than the published prices.

- Today, public four-year universities have a published price of about $21,000 per year on average—but the average student pays less than $15,000 per year after grants and scholarships, a $6,000 discount. For private four-year universities, the published price averages $48,500 and the average student pays just over $27,000 per year, a $21,500 discount.

- Saving for retirement is critical and should take priority over funding your student's higher education; put on your oxygen mask first!

- There are a variety of ways to save for college, including 529 savings plans which allow you to invest tax-free for educational expenses. The most important thing is to start saving early. One dollar in college savings can grow into many dollars in debt avoided.

CHAPTER TWO

Early High School: Preparing for the Process

During the first two years of high school, college may still seem far off in the distance—but it's actually a reality that's approaching faster than you may think. Just as your student's courses, grades, and activities will influence their future path to college, so will your finances. Early high school is the time to lay some of the groundwork that will position you strategically for the best financial aid support when your student is ready to apply to college.

In this chapter you'll learn more about some of the basics to student financial aid, including the Free Application for Federal Student Aid (FAFSA), the College Board's CSS Profile, and the Expected Family Contribution (EFC). We'll also review different eligibility categories for student financial aid, including need-based and merit-based aid as well as the various types of financial aid you can expect to receive. We'll mention financial aid opportunities for immigrants, children of immigrants, and international students, too.

Finally, setting expectations are key, so we'll discuss why these early high school years are a good time for you and your future college student to begin setting financial expectations about who will pay for college.

TYPES OF COLLEGE COSTS

Recall that we defined a college's **published cost of attendance** as the estimated budget for a student for one year of study. Here are the largest components of that cost of attendance:

Tuition

Tuition is what colleges and universities charge for instruction, including classes, seminars, and workshops. Essentially, tuition covers your classes: the education portion of your higher education experience. At many colleges, tuition is broken down by credit or credit hour with a specific fee per credit. The requirement for a bachelor's degree is universal: students need to earn 120 credits to graduate. Some colleges may charge a flat tuition rate per semester or academic year, covering a typical range of credits.

In-State Tuition

In-state tuition refers to the tuition cost for a student who is a resident of the same state as the public college or university they plan to attend. For example, a high school senior living in Milton, Pennsylvania, would pay in-state tuition at Penn State University. In-state tuition is typically cheaper than out-of-state tuition. Some states offer in-state tuition to out-of-state students; more on this in Chapter Three.

Out-of-State Tuition

Out-of-state tuition refers to the tuition cost for a student who does not live in the same state as the public college or university they attend. For example, a high school senior living in New York City would pay out-of-state tuition at Penn State University. Out-of-state tuition typically is more expensive than in-state tuition but generally less than private college tuition.

Private College Tuition

Private college tuition is the cost private colleges charge for teaching and instruction. Tuition at private colleges and universities can be charged by credit or by a flat rate, as with public universities. There is no difference in published price for in-state and out-of-state students at private colleges, though there may be opportunities like special scholarships for local students.

Fees

Each school will have its own fee structure, so be sure to delve into the fine print to understand the fees charged at the colleges that interest you to avoid any surprises later. In some cases, tuition and fees are presented together—in others, fees will be itemized (and some may be able to be waived, though many are required).

Room and Board

"Room" is where you reside (e.g. a dorm), and "board" would include the cost of food (e.g. a meal plan). You may be required to live on campus and purchase a meal plan for some or all of the years you are in college. Typically, colleges will share an average figure for room and board but should also be able to provide detail on the variety of options (such as where you could save money, or spend more for that fancy dorm!).

Other Expenses

In addition to tuition, fees, and room and board, a true cost of attendance will also include estimates for things like books and supplies, travel, and other living expenses. Colleges may break these down in different ways (or omit them altogether), but you'll certainly incur some additional expenses in those categories.

In a later chapter, we'll cover how to come up with a robust budget based on your particular situation that includes those expenses and other costs that could come up in the course of your studies. For now, the cost of attendance — or even the total tuition plus fees and room and board — is a good starting point.

TYPES OF FINANCIAL AID

In the snapshot on college price, we talked about the **net price**—the price you'll actually pay, which is different for everyone and for every school. So, how do you get from a **cost of attendance** to your personal net price?

The answer is financial aid. Here, we'll use "financial aid" as an umbrella term that includes grants and scholarships from the college, including merit aid. Loans and work-study that the college approves can also be considered forms of financial aid—but they are not "free money," so to speak, since you have to pay them back or work for them. More on this later.

More than 80% of college students receive some form of financial aid, according to the latest data from the National Center for Education Statistics. Depending on your family finances, demographics, and financial need, and your student's academic record and extracurriculars, you may be able to apply or be considered for all types of financial aid.

The tricky thing about financial aid is that you probably will get a different amount of financial aid from every college you apply to. In the coming sections we will help you figure out how much you're likely to receive so that you can build a college list with schools that will be generous to you.

GRANTS AND SCHOLARSHIPS

Grants and scholarships are "free money"—money allocated for higher education expenses that does not need to be repaid. Both grants and scholarships can come from federal or state governments, or directly from a two- or four-year college or university. (They can also come from businesses, religious groups, civic associations, and nonprofit organizations—we'll call these "private scholarships.") Many grants and scholarships are awarded on a competitive basis and can either be one-time gifts or recur over the duration of one's education.

FEDERAL LOANS

Student loans are funds allocated for higher education expenses and will need to be repaid, with interest, after graduation. There are two types of student loans: federal and private.

Federal student loans, administered by the U.S. Department of Education, fall into four categories:

- *Subsidized*: Allocated for undergraduate students with financial need. The term "subsidized" means that they do not accrue interest while the student is enrolled in college.
- *Unsubsidized*: Allocated for undergraduate, graduate, and professional students regardless of financial need.
- *Direct PLUS loans*: Allocated for graduate or professional students, or parents of dependent undergraduate students.
- *Direct Consolidation loans*: Allocated for students who

would like to combine all their federal student loans into one account (after college).

Federal student loans have lower fixed interest rates than private student loans. Additionally, federal student loan servicers may have more flexibility regarding repayment plans, including deferment and income-based repayment plans, compared to private student loan lenders. We'll discuss loans in more depth in Chapter Four.

Generally, a financial aid letter from the college will show the subsidized and unsubsidized federal student loans you are eligible for. The others—including Parent PLUS loans or private loans—will be pursued by you at your discretion. Since private loans originate from private institutions, such as local banks, national banks, and credit unions, and aren't connected to colleges, they can't be considered financial aid. The same goes for Parent PLUS loans, which require additional verification to borrow.

WORK-STUDY

The Federal Work-Study program funds part-time jobs at participating colleges and universities around the country, enabling students to earn a pre-set amount of money each semester to put toward education and living expenses.

Ideally, work-study jobs are intended to provide on-the-job work experience that relates to the student's major, although each student's work-study experience will vary based on campus need, job openings, and hiring practices. Federal work-study jobs are available to both part-time and full-time undergraduate, graduate, and professional students who demonstrate financial need. Although anyone can seek work during college, including on-campus, work-study is officially part of some financial aid packages as there are funds set aside for a certain number of needy students.

"NEED-BASED" VS. "MERIT-BASED" FINANCIAL AID

Financial aid is divided into two categories: need-based and merit-based. The distinction between the two types has largely to do with eligibility and how they are funded.

Almost all financial aid provided by federal and state governments is need-based financial aid. Colleges award both need-based aid and merit-based aid. Many different private sponsors award scholarships with diverse eligibility requirements, ranging from religious groups, community groups, cultural organizations, national foundations such as the Bill & Melinda Gates Foundation and the Coca Cola Scholars Foundation, and private individuals, such as wealthy alumni who endow scholarship programs for their alma maters.

Need-Based Financial Aid

Need-based financial aid is awarded strictly based on a student's financial profile, which considers the student's family assets and income, not the student's academic merit. (Colleges, of course, will consider academic merit when deciding whether or not a student should be admitted—but it doesn't factor into this aid calculation.) Need-based aid can include a combination of grants, scholarships, subsidized student loans, and work-study.

With the exception of the Iraq and Afghanistan Service Grants, most federal aid is need-based aid, with the federal government determining eligibility solely from a given family's finances.

Merit-Based Financial Aid

Merit-based financial aid is based on a student's accomplishment and talents in academics, athletics, arts, and volunteer or charitable works. Merit scholarships are typically, though not always, need-blind, meaning that a student's financial profile is not considered when determining their candidacy. They sometimes require an application or selection via committee. Often merit scholarships act like discounts, meant to make the college more attractive to high-quality students.

Some sponsors of merit scholarships only evaluate grade-point averages, test scores, or class rank, while others may consider academic performance in addition to teacher recommendations and community involvement. For example:

- Individual academic departments at a college may have scholarships specifically for promising students in a given major.
- Some colleges automatically grant scholarships for achievements such as a particular class rank, test scores, or GPA.

APPLYING FOR FINANCIAL AID

Applying for financial aid is done alongside applying to college. You'll need to provide your financial information, using the right forms, and you may need to meet a special deadline. Even if you think you make too much money for financial aid, you should still take the time to complete the FAFSA.

The Free Application for Federal Student Aid (FAFSA)

The Free Application for Federal Student Aid, also known as the FAFSA, is the government application that financial aid offices at colleges and universities. Community colleges and Ivy League institutions alike (as well as everything in between) use this form to determine eligibility for financial aid and what kind of financial aid package to offer. The FAFSA collects personal and financial information from parents and their dependent children, and at your direction delivers that information to the schools to which you have applied.

Expected Family Contribution (EFC)

The Expected Family Contribution is essentially the minimum dollar amount that the government thinks your family could reasonably afford to pay for one academic year. Your EFC is determined by your entries on the FAFSA form. Confusingly, the EFC is not the amount of money you will actually have to pay for college—and it's not the amount of financial aid you will receive either. It's a number that is used by the college to decide your financial aid.

Your EFC is the most important number to know when starting your college search because it tells you whether or not colleges will consider you for need-based financial aid. In the next chapter we will tell you how to get your EFC and how to interpret the number.

CSS Profile

The College Board's CSS Profile is an additional, separate application document required by many private colleges. The CSS Profile asks for more detailed financial information than the FAFSA and is used to award non-federal ("institutional," or from the college) need-based financial aid. The form was developed by the College Board, but colleges can customize the application and formula, so the dollar amounts offered by individual colleges who use the Profile may differ.

As one college consultant put it, "the FAFSA is processed by a computer (no human eye sees this data), while the CSS Profile and the FAFSA results (the EFC) are evaluated by the professional financial aid officers at colleges and universities."

HOW FINANCIAL NEED IS CALCULATED

Now that we've established the essential terms you'll need to know for the financial aid process, we'll get deeper into how your need is calculated.

FAFSA Basics

For a given academic year, the U.S. Department of Education allows students to submit the FAFSA forms between October of the previous academic year and June of the current academic year, with the federal FAFSA deadline that same June. For example, the FAFSA for the 2020-21 academic year was made available on October 1, 2019, with a federal deadline of midnight CST on June 30, 2020.

The information you'll provide is from what is called "prior prior year" so that you have access to a full year of financial information when filling it out in October. This means that for a student going from high school straight to college, the tax year starting January of their sophomore year and concluding in December of their junior year is the first tax year to "count" for financial aid.

For this college academic year ...	You can submit the FAFSA starting ...	Using tax information from ...
July 2020-June 2021	October 1, 2019	2018
July 2021-June 2022	October 1, 2020	2019
July 2022-June 2023	October 1, 2021	2020

Adapted from StudentAid.gov

The most important factors in the FAFSA formula are your household gross income and the number of children a family has in college in a given year. Assets are also a factor, though less significant. Note that financial need may change year to year, based on variables in your family's income and assets.

WHICH ASSETS COUNT ON THE FAFSA
Parents are expected to use up to 5.64% of their available assets each year to pay for college. However, not all assets are considered by the FAFSA; for example, home equity is not.

Assets that *will* affect your EFC:
- Balances in your basic checking and savings accounts
- CDs
- Brokerage accounts
- Money market accounts
- Investment real estate (*not* your primary residence)
- Stocks
- Bonds
- Mutual funds
- ETFs
- Commodities
- 529 college savings and prepaid plans (including those in siblings' names, as parent assets)

If your student has a trust fund, that must also be reported, even if the funds are not currently available to them to use.

Assets that will *not* affect your EFC as they are not reported on the FAFSA:

- Any retirement assets, such as a 401K, 403B, IRAs, SEP, SIMPLE, profiting sharing, pensions, and Roth IRAs
- The value of your family's primary residence
- The value of a family farm
- Any family-run small businesses with fewer than 100 people working there
- Life insurance policies
- Any personal possessions

PARENTAL VS. STUDENT ASSETS

Parental assets and student assets are treated differently on the FAFSA, and parent assets count less when their dependents are applying to college. The first reason: the FAFSA's Federal Methodology contains provisions for what's called an "asset protection allowance" in an attempt to ensure that at least some of parents' assets are excluded from the EFC calculation. The asset protection allowance is set annually by the U.S. Department of Education and is meant to help families save for retirement, without completely emptying their savings to help children pay for college.

Parents are given a protection allowance of $30,000 to $60,000, based on the age of the oldest parent living in the student's house, and the number of parents. Note this protection is only offered to parents of dependent college students, and not to students themselves.

The second reason parent assets count less is that the formula weighs them lower than student assets. Parent assets are assessed at most at 5.64%—meaning for every $1,000 of assets above the protection allowance, your EFC will go up less than $60. Student assets (including cash savings in the student's name) are not subject to a protection allowance so all reportable assets are included in the calculation. They are also assessed at a much higher rate of 20%. For every $1,000 of student assets, then, their EFC will go up $200!

The FAFSA formula generally does not change from year to year; however, inputs such as asset protection allowances and asset conversion rates are subject to annual revision.

CSS Profile Basics and How it Differs from FAFSA

The CSS Profile provides colleges with a much more thorough and accurate picture of a family's true financial background than the FAFSA does. The CSS Profile requires not only the "prior prior year" tax filings, but also the last and current year estimate. It considers a longer list of assets than the FAFSA when evaluating your financial need.

The CSS Profile is considered differently by every institution that reviews it, and different aspects may be weighted according to the individual policies of that college. For example, recording any retirement assets is a requirement for completing the CSS Profile, although most financial services departments at schools don't consider it in their final review.

The CSS Profile considers the money you have, but also the expenses your family is responsible for. The Profile asks questions about your medical history as well as your family's, any debts incurred by you or them, where your home is located, and business expenses you may not have otherwise been able to clarify on the FAFSA.

Below is the information that the CSS Profile collects for universities, in addition to all the same information that the FAFSA collects.

Different requests between the FAFSA and CSS Profile:

- *Income, taxes, and exemptions*: the CSS Profile requests the past two years of tax filings in addition to the current year estimate.
- *Family business/farm*: the FAFSA only asks for information if your family business or farm exceeds 100 employees, whereas the CSS Profile requests it regardless of the size of the business.

Categories included on the CSS Profile that are not required on the FAFSA:

- Home equity in primary residence
- Trust funds
- Medical spending accounts (including HSAs and FSAs)
- Siblings' assets held in parent's name
- Siblings' K-12 private school tuition
- Total retirement savings
- Non-retirement annuities
- Other valuables

How Will Your Home Equity Affect Financial Aid?

Because home equity is often a family's largest asset, it can have a large impact if used in financial aid calculations. This explains why similar schools might look very different in cost after a financial aid package is offered.

Only colleges that take the CSS Profile will know the value of the equity in your home. For those that take it into account, some will simply assume a percentage of the value could be drawn on for college and add that percentage to your EFC—as with other parent assets on the FAFSA and CSS Profile. Other CSS Profile schools will cap the home equity value in their financial aid calculations based on a multiplier of total parent income.

Some CSS Profile schools omit the home equity in their calculations altogether despite having access to the information via the form. Stanford, a CSS Profile school, announced in December of 2018 that it would stop capping home equity and begin excluding it completely from its financial aid calculations. There is an emerging trend among selective colleges toward excluding home equity in order to not unfairly penalize middle- and upper-middle-class homeowners with moderate income in expensive geographic areas. Harvard, Princeton, and MIT also exclude it from their considerations, for example. If Stanford is any indication, trustee boards for top tier universities are likely to see removing home equity from financial aid calculations as the next step in enhancing already robust financial aid programs. This could be a huge help for middle-class families.

For example, a family with a household income of $100,000 and a home equity value of $300,000 would not have their EFC impacted by their home at all at Stanford.

But if a college counted the home equity, the EFC could go up around $15,000—meaning your financial aid could decrease $15,000 per year. This is because assets are assessed at around 5%, and 5% of $300,000 is $15,000.

If a college "capped" the home equity value at 2x income, the formula would count the home equity value as $200,000 instead of $300,000. So the EFC could go up $10,000 and financial aid could decrease by the same amount.

OTHER CIRCUMSTANCES THAT AFFECT FINANCIAL AID

Divorced Parents

As you've no doubt gathered by now, the financial aid process is tricky. Applications for aid become even more convoluted as family structures become more diverse.

If parents are divorced or legally separated and don't live together, the FAFSA only requires information from the custodial parent. According to the FAFSA guidelines, the only parent who needs to do any reporting is the parent with "whom [the student] lived more during the past 12 months." If you lived with both parents an equal amount of time, the FAFSA will require the information from the parent who provided the most financial support to the student.

If the custodial parent has remarried, the step-parent is required to report their financials as well.

However, when filling out the CSS Profile, the amount of information required on your application will depend on each institution's expectations. Some colleges only want the information from the custodial parent, while others require the information of both biological parents regardless of divorce or separation. In that case, the parents will create separate profiles and complete separate applications. The CSS Profile also requires financial information to be reported by a step-parent if the custodial parent has remarried.

For 529 plans, only the custodial parent must list information about the 529 plan as an asset on the FAFSA. (For the CSS Profile, again, the reporting requirements vary from school to school.) A 529 plan should only be reported as an asset on the FAFSA if it belongs to the custodial parent or the student. If the 529 plan is in the name of the non-custodial parent, it should not be reported.

Be aware that if a non-custodial parent distributes funds from the 529 plan to the student, it will be reported as untaxed income. This will have a negative impact on the need-based aid the student will receive for the following year. The best workaround for this is to only use the funds in that 529 plan in the last year of college (as there will be no need for aid the year after graduation).

Independent vs. Dependent Students

In the above sections we have mostly assumed that students are "dependents" of their parents for the sake of financial aid. Some conditions for financial aid are different if a student is financially independent or not supported by their parents financially.

The acceptable conditions to qualify as an independent student for the purposes of financial aid are strict. You must be one or several of the following:

- At least 24 years old
- Married
- A graduate or professional student
- A veteran or on active duty as a member of the armed forces
- An orphan
- A ward of the court
- Someone with legal dependents other than a spouse
- An emancipated minor
- Someone who is homeless or at risk of becoming homeless

If a student does not qualify as independent but their parents refuse to share their financial information, the student can still file the FAFSA but will need to note the circumstances—and may not be eligible for federal financial aid.

Immigration Status

A student's immigration status may make them ineligible for specific financial aid opportunities. The key categories are the following:

- Naturalized citizens have the same rights and opportunities to financial aid opportunities as native-born citizens.

- Permanent immigrants, including lawful permanent residents, refugees, and asylum recipients, are eligible for all three types of federal student aid: grants, work-study, and loans in addition to other forms of aid.

- Temporary residents, which includes foreign students on a visa, are not eligible.

- Immigrants with discretionary status, including undocumented immigrants, are not eligible for federal student aid but do have aid opportunities from some individual states, colleges, and private sources.

CAN I REDUCE MY EXPECTED FAMILY CONTRIBUTION?

The early high school years are the perfect time to speak to an accountant or financial advisor to avoid financial moves that could unexpectedly impact your aid. As we have discussed, considerations such as the following can have meaningful consequences:

- In whose name an asset is held (parent, student, or other relative)
- When distributions are received from a 529 plan outside of the immediate family
- Income fluctuations year to year (from employment or investments)
- Your home equity

Be wary of schemes that promise to help you hide your assets or reduce your EFC through complex or drastic financial maneuvers. Even setting aside the ethical implications, it will be a better use of your time to focus on finding affordable colleges that will be generous with families like yours than to try to game a complex system and eke out a few thousand dollars.

For example, lawmakers and college officials are alert to a scam where parents gave up guardianship of their high school aged children to render them independent students without assets. Some colleges have even said they will not provide financial aid to students they determine have used such dubious approaches to obtain financial aid for which they are otherwise ineligible.

SETTING FINANCIAL EXPECTATIONS WITH YOUR CHILD

Paying for college is often best approached as a family discussion and a family endeavor—and the first couple of years of high school aren't too early to begin this conversation.

This may be one of the first times you have had frank discussions about finances with your student around what is and is not affordable. Some parents make it clear to children that their college choice will depend on whichever school will cost the least. Other parents present more of a cost-benefit analysis; for example, explaining to their student that they could also afford a car if they choose the less costly option of a four-year public college over a private college. Some parents encourage their student to work full-time in the summer to earn a certain amount in order to make college work financially. Perhaps you *could* pay for college in full, but you want your student to have some financial responsibility—so you expect them to contribute a certain amount or take a small loan (even if it's from you, interest free).

These are difficult conversations to have—because many high school students are not long-term planners and don't generally have extensive experience with these financial concepts. Here are some of the discussion topics you should introduce early with your student.

Acting like a Consumer

As you have seen, the financial aid system is complicated—that is in part because colleges and universities are trying to allocate their dollars fairly so that families can afford their education. But it's also because colleges and universities have their own business considerations to keep in mind. Different students are asked to pay different prices so that the college can maximize its revenue while admitting a diverse class.

Because of demographic, economic, and other trends, many colleges are having difficulties with their business model. You may have seen news stories about small colleges shuttering their doors because their enrollments were down and they could no longer make it work. As a result, competition for students is getting more intense. Colleges need and want you to say yes! This is why, as we saw in Chapter One, net prices are not actually growing as fast as the published prices. There is often more discounting available.

We believe that families should act like consumers in the college process and know that they have buying power—in other words, while you're applying to get in, you should also be aware that you're offering something to the college that they want and need. When you are empowered with that information you'll be able to find the school that will offer the best value.

Who Pays for College

As with most everything, who pays for college and how much they

45

pay varies family to family and household to household. Though there is no right answer for how you and your family should divide the cost of school, you may be interested in some of the available data to give you an idea of trends happening across the United States.

In a recent study, *How America Pays for College (2019)*, researchers from Sallie Mae surveyed college-going students and their families and found the following:

- 43% of college costs were covered by family savings and income (30% from the parents' income and savings, and 13% from students').
- Both parents and students borrow money to cover education costs. On average, parents borrow 10% of the total amount due while students borrow 14%.
- 31% of the cost of college is covered by scholarships and grants won by the student.
- The final 2% is covered by relatives and friends.

According to the same study, 12% of families say parents made the decision on their own and 24% say students made the decision about paying for college on their own. Fifty-one percent of families make the decision together.

Of course, the numbers in this study show trends, not requirements—a good conversation starter about how to cover the cost of school.

What's the Value of a College Education?

Choosing a college is a big decision, one that encompasses not only a family's finances but also your student's and your collective values and future goals. College is where critical reasoning and life skills are developed, career paths are forged, and lifelong friendships established.

But given that it's such a big financial decision, one that could either lead to a great return on investment or a long-term struggle with student loan debt, families will want to approach the college decision in as level-headed a manner as possible.

For now, get your student acquainted with the concept of "return on investment." A higher cost requires a higher gain to achieve the same ROI as a lower-cost investment. Getting a college education leads to higher earnings and to lower unemployment rates in the long-term. It also provides many other benefits that may be less tangible and whose value is specific to the student—factors like campus culture, diversity, and opportunities for extracurriculars or professional development. Encourage your student to start thinking about what's most important to your family in the college decision.

TAKEAWAYS

- Begin to lay the groundwork for how your family will make the financial aspects of the college decision. Discuss how you plan to position yourself for the best price, who will pay for college, and what outcomes you want from your college investment.
- Your price for a college can depend on your family's financial situation (need-based) as well as your academic or other strengths (merit-based). The amount of need-based and merit-based aid available varies by college.
- Everyone applying for financial aid must fill out the FAFSA, which asks for financial information about income and assets.
- Private colleges often also require the CSS Profile, which

asks for more detailed financial information than the FAFSA.

- The Expected Family Contribution, or the amount your family can afford to pay for college, is calculated differently on the FAFSA and the CSS Profile. This is the number that colleges use to calculate your aid.

CHAPTER THREE

Junior Year: Refining Your List

By junior year of high school, preparing to apply to colleges becomes more real. Chances are your student will have heard about specific colleges from peers and teachers and is beginning to envision their future choices. Students (and parents, too) can be susceptible to forming opinions about which schools are desirable based on relatively little information, but we believe that building a list of potential colleges that will best fit academically, socially, and financially is better done systematically, as an informed consumer. This chapter will help you do just that.

Junior year is important academically because it is the last full year colleges will see on a high school transcript. It's also the year in which financial expectations may start to meet reality. As you start your college research, you should factor in the financial research with your research on all the other characteristics of colleges. Staying aligned with your student this year will ensure that the colleges they fall in love with and aspire to will also be colleges you feel confident you can afford and have a good financial outcome.

In this chapter we'll explain how to figure out what colleges will be generous with families like yours. First, we will look at your EFC introduced in Chapter Two. We delve into what types of aid you may be eligible for and how to tell. We'll also explain some of the many factors that college administrators weigh when offering a financial aid package. The second part of the chapter gives you information to begin building a list of best financial-fit colleges.

HOW FINANCIAL NEED–BASED AID IS CALCULATED

Understanding Demonstrated Financial Need

Recall that your EFC is the amount the FAFSA calculates that you can contribute annually to college. Demonstrated need is how many dollars, according to the FAFSA, that the student would need *in addition to their EFC* to attend a particular school, per year.

Let us briefly walk through the math. It's a bit complicated, but if you understand this section it will set the best foundation for you to maximize your aid and reduce your cost of college.

Four main factors determine federal aid:

1. Year in school
2. Enrollment status (i.e., full-time or part-time)
3. Cost of attendance (COA)
4. Expected Family Contribution (EFC)

The EFC subtracted from COA equals the student's demonstrated financial need. This is what the student could require in student financial aid to cover the cost of a specific school. Think about it as the gap between what the government says you "can" pay (your EFC) and what you need (the cost of attendance). After paying the amount of your EFC, what will still need to be paid?

For example, if the cost of attendance at a university is $50,000 per year, a family with an EFC of $20,000 will have a financial need of $30,000. This is the gap between what the government calculates they could pay and what the college's sticker price is.

Just because this family's financial need is $30,000, though, does not mean the college will give them $30,000 in financial aid. More on this below.

The Variability of Financial Need
All parts of the financial need equation are variable, meaning that your financial need could vary drastically from school to school and year to year. The published cost of different colleges are different, of course. Your EFC is also variable, depending on how your financial situation changes. For instance, the amount that your family makes every year might change. You may withdraw from your retirement plan. Perhaps another sibling started college. All of this and more will change the EFC value year to year.

Financial Need and Income Level
Low-income families tend to get more financial aid than high-income families. In theory, the less money you have to contribute to your student's education, the lower your expected contribution. In some cases, the EFC for very low-income students can be $0. A lower EFC means the demonstrated need would be higher. For example, a $0-EFC student applying to the $50,000 per year school mentioned above would have a financial need of the full cost of $50,000.

Even if your EFC seems high (and in many cases it will feel high to you) it does not mean you won't receive financial aid. The U.S. Department of Education's *National Postsecondary Student Aid Study* showed that in 2015-16 just over 96% of undergraduate students with family incomes of less than $20,000 received financial aid in some form, while nearly 79% of students in families making more than $100,000 received aid.

Though the incomes of these families varied drastically, the vast majority of both groups—more than three-quarters in both cases—received financial aid.

There are many reasons why that might be. Consider the two students below applying to different colleges. Though their EFCs are very different, the financial need for both students is the same. This is why many high-income students also find themselves eligible for at least some financial aid.

	Student A, College X	Student B, College Y
Cost of Attendance	15,000	50,000
(-) EFC	-5,000	-40,000
(=) Financial Need	10,000	10,000

Percent of Need Met

Colleges have varying amounts of financial aid available to offer students. This means that the amount of financial aid you will be offered will vary in part based on each college's resources.

Once your school receives your demonstrated financial need information from the FAFSA (or CSS Profile), the admissions and financial aid departments will determine how much money they will give you to cover that need.

In the best cases, 100% of your financial need will be covered by the school of your choice. Indeed, there are a number of schools all over the United States that cover the entire amount of demonstrated financial need for incoming students through an aid package that combines scholarships, grants, federal loans, and work-study. Most schools, though, can't guarantee this kind of coverage. Instead, they only cover a percentage of your financial need.

The portion of the gap that the school covers is your need met. This is a percent from 0% to 100%. Let's look at Student B from the prior page.

	Student B, College Y
Cost of Attendance	50,000
(-) EFC	-40,000
(=) Financial Need	10,000
Financial Aid Given	5,000
Need Met	5,000/10,000 = 50%

Although most schools can't promise 100% coverage to all of their students, many still aim to cover the majority of that need. Even if a college doesn't fully cover student financial need, it doesn't mean that they don't offer any aid. They might offer large merit scholarships to students they want to encourage to attend.

Perhaps more importantly, you might not feel your EFC is feasible—so even if a college were to meet all of your "need" it would still be a stretch. More on this below.

Need-Blind vs. Need-Aware Admission

Families often wonder how their financial need factors into admissions decisions. Some colleges consider a family's ability to pay when making an admissions decision, while some don't.

NEED-BLIND SCHOOLS

Need-blind admissions policies do *not* account for socioeconomic status when deciding whether or not to accept an individual student. A student's financial aid package is formulated only after the acceptance decision is made.

Only the wealthiest schools are typically need-blind—examples include Amherst College and Brown University. Although the idea is that need-blind is truly fair because it admits students on merits only, some argue that "fair" is a relative term because the wealthiest schools tend to make admissions decisions based on factors that correlate highly to student wealth, such as SAT scores or expensive extracurricular activities.

NEED-AWARE SCHOOLS

Most schools cannot afford to be need-blind because they rely on tuition revenue to fund their operations. If they accept students who will need significant financial aid, they need to also accept students who have the ability to pay more.

Need-aware admissions policies *do* factor a student's ability to pay for college into admissions decisions. This doesn't mean that it's the first or most important factor in the acceptance decision, but financial status could play a role.

Need-aware is controversial because it may be perceived to favor students who are "full pay" or can better afford to pay a higher proportion of tuition. But need-aware is for most colleges a matter of survival—and many colleges aim to offer financial aid that enables lower-income students to attend. Colleges don't typically advertise that they are need-aware. If a school doesn't say that it's need-blind, it probably isn't!

Also remember that being need-blind does not mean a school will be able to fulfill financial need. In many cases need-blind schools will not meet full need of applicants, and so lower-income students could be better off at need aware schools with more generous financial aid packages.

MERIT-BASED FINANCIAL AID (SCHOLARSHIPS)

To recap from Chapter Two, merit scholarships, unlike need-based financial aid, are awarded to students based on academic or other merit, such as athletics or community involvement rather than demonstrated financial need. Merit-based aid is often (but not always) need-blind.

Families who see that their EFC is higher than they are able or willing to pay for college, or who are considering colleges that are less generous with need-based aid, should seek schools with generous merit scholarships.

Where to Find Merit-Based Scholarships

The vast majority of merit scholarships are provided by colleges directly. Colleges award merit scholarships as a method of attracting the most qualified students by competing on price against similar colleges.

Not all colleges award merit scholarships. The most selective universities tend to reserve their funds for financial need-based aid. Colleges also vary in their generosity with merit scholarships. Some may award many small merit scholarships to lots of applicants, while others might award larger scholarships only to the most qualified candidates.

Applying for Merit-Based Scholarships

The application process for every merit scholarship is different. Some colleges that award merit-based aid allow your college application to double as your merit scholarship application, while other schools require submission of a separate application. In some cases, you need to submit your application by an earlier date in order to be considered, so keep that in mind. You should be able to check the college admissions website for this information or call the financial aid office directly.

Additionally, if your student obtains a merit scholarship, make sure they understand what is required to keep the scholarship. Schools and private scholarship sponsors typically require recipients to maintain a specified minimum GPA for as many years as the scholarship is granted, possibly in addition to other requirements. Also note that not all scholarships are awarded for every year of college. Some merit-based aid programs only provide assistance for the first year of school, while other programs award decreasing amounts of money beyond freshman year. Many merit-based scholarships are one-time awards with no possibility of annual renewal.

Why Private Scholarships are the Wrong Place to Focus

While merit-based scholarships from the college are somewhat built in to the application process, the process of applying for non-school-based (private) merit scholarships is typically much more varied and onerous.

In addition to a general application, private scholarship sponsors may require candidates to submit written essays, obtain letters of recommendation, or sit for interviews. Applying for private merit scholarships, if approached indiscriminately, can almost feel like a full-time job! We recommend focusing on merit scholarships awarded by colleges, since those awards tend to be the largest and require the least amount of additional work to obtain.

If you do pursue private scholarships, it's best to prioritize the ones for which you are most qualified. Otherwise you may expend a significant amount of time and energy on the scholarship application process but ultimately reap very little financial reward.

Another important risk of private scholarships is that it could impact your financial aid. Because of something called scholarship displacement, receiving a private scholarship can result in your school reducing or rescinding other forms of financial aid. The justification is that since you have received additional funding, your financial need is less than when you applied. The policies on this vary college to college.

FINANCIAL AID AT DIFFERENT TYPES OF COLLEGES

While you will soon be researching individual colleges, it's helpful to understand some broad rules of thumb about how pricing and financial aid works at different types of institutions. This way you'll be able to easily make some assumptions about the types of colleges and universities you want to focus on in your search.

Ivy League Universities

Ivy League schools don't grant merit scholarships because, as one admissions counselor put it, "All our admitted students qualify for merit-based scholarships; the differences between them come down to need."

Almost all Ivy League universities use the CSS Profile in addition to the FAFSA as a major component of their need calculation (Princeton does not). Still, even utilizing the same data, individual institutions will give different amounts of financial aid based on their own estimates of financial need (what they do with the data). For example, some Ivy League schools will use home equity in different ways in their financial aid calculations.

Note that many middle-class students receive financial aid once they are admitted to an Ivy League college. As a general rule, as long as a student's EFC is below their expected COA, they can expect to receive financial aid. These schools meet 100% of financial need.

Students from low-income backgrounds with high financial need may be offered financial aid that covers the full cost of tuition, supplies, and even living expenses. The threshold for need to receive this "full ride" can vary by institution.

Public vs. Private Colleges and Universities

Are state schools cheaper than private colleges? The answer is not as obvious as you might think.

The defining difference between public and private institutions is how they're funded—and this affects the costs for students. Public schools are funded mainly by state governments, while private colleges are supported primarily by their own endowment funds and students' tuition fees. Both may also receive contributions from individual donors.

COST OF ATTENDANCE

The published price of public colleges and universities is almost always less than that of private colleges. Because public universities are heavily subsidized by state governments, they are able to charge lower tuition rates to students. In-state residents receive favorable tuition rates at public universities based on the premise that their tax dollars fund the state governments. Private colleges, on the other hand, have higher published costs because they rely more heavily on students' tuition payments to cover operating expenses.

Tuition, Fees, Room and Board ('18-'19)	
Private Nonprofit Four-Year	$48,510
Public Four-Year (Out-of-State)	$37,430
Public Four-Year (In-State)	$21,370

Source: *College Board*

AVAILABILITY OF FINANCIAL AID

Although private colleges and universities may have higher published prices, they frequently offer more substantial tuition discounts than public universities. Both public and private colleges can provide federal financial aid to students, but private institutions typically have more money available to fund additional grants and scholarships. Private colleges' ability to offer more attractive financial aid packages can sometimes make them more affordable than public universities despite their more expensive sticker price.

FINANCIAL AID AT PUBLIC UNIVERSITIES FOR OUT-OF-STATE STUDENTS

Out-of-state students are less likely to get financial aid from public universities—something many families overlook. In many cases private universities can be more affordable after financial aid than going to a public university out-of-state.

> Laura wanted to go to a large school in California. She lived in Atlanta and with scholarships the University of Georgia would cost around $18,000. Laura also applied to several public universities in California. While she received some aid, the net prices ranged from $32,000 to $38,000—with no further scholarships available. She would have to pay nearly double what she would have paid in-state to go to a public college in California.

That said, here are some ways that out-of-state students can get discounted tuition at public universities.

- *Regional Consortia or State Reciprocity Agreements:* According to the Cornell Higher Education Research Institute (CHERI), of the 149 public research and doctorate institutions in the U.S., 61 of them reported participating in a tuition reciprocity program of some sort, through which qualifying students can attend some out-of-state public institutions at much more affordable (sometimes even in-state) rates. Some states have smaller reciprocity programs or offer flexibility in determining who qualifies for in-state tuition. Other states even have flexible definitions of residency for students living in border counties of a neighboring state. For example, the Minnesota-Wisconsin tuition reciprocity agreement allows Wisconsin residents to attend public universities in Minnesota and receive in-state tuition. Under the New Mexico-Colorado tuition reciprocity agreement, students from either New Mexico or Colorado can attend public institutions at each other's state at in-state tuition rates.

- *Nonresident Scholarships:* Another way to receive in-state tuition is to search for programs specific to an individual university. Most public universities have scholarships specifically for nonresident students. Try searching the college website for scholarship programs that waive nonresident tuition as a part of their award. And don't overlook diversity or legacy scholarships, which may emphasize qualities other than academic excellence alone.

- *Special Circumstances:* Some schools and state-wide policies waive out-of-state tuition based on special circumstances. For example, active military personnel and their dependents are eligible for in-state tuition where they currently live regardless of their resident status.

HOW TO ESTIMATE YOUR COSTS FOR SPECIFIC COLLEGES

As discussed in Chapter Two, you won't fill out your official FAFSA until October of your senior year—and you won't get your official financial aid information from the college until after you apply and are accepted. But it's important you not be in the dark until then about what you'll perhaps need to pay for college. Here are a few recommended tools to use as you do your research.

Estimating (and Understanding) Your EFC

There is a tool called the FAFSA4caster, from the U.S. Department of Education, which you can use to get an estimate of your EFC. It will also show you the federal financial aid you might be eligible for at a given college, including Pell Grants, work-study, and federal loans. Keep in mind that the aid estimates shown by FAFSA4caster are incomplete because they don't include money from your state or college (need-based or merit aid), or private scholarships. So, it's best used to get a sense of your EFC before senior year.

A common refrain from parents who see their EFC number: "There's no way I could pay that much per year!" Here are some of the most common reasons your EFC might be high:

- *Your household income is high.* For most students, a high household income will be the reason for a high EFC. EFC increases as the family's household income increases, holding all other factors constant. The EFC formula considers both parents' incomes and the student's income, with higher-income families expected to contribute more to their student's education. The formula also increases if the student in question has a higher income.

- *You have a lot of non-retirement financial assets (excluding your family home).* If your family has accumulated wealth and investments, your EFC can be high, even if your family's income is low. This includes checking and savings accounts, stocks and bonds, and even the student's 529 savings plan.

- *You live in a low-tax state.* Because state taxes can contribute greatly to the cost of living, the EFC formula grants higher state tax allowances to families from states with higher tax rates. A higher allowance results in a lower EFC, because it is deducted from your income in the formula.

- *You have fewer children attending college.* The more members of a household attending college, the lower each college student's expected EFC. Note: if, in future years, you'll have multiple children in college at the same time, your EFC can drop significantly.

Once you have your approximate EFC, you'll know what your price will be at minimum for most colleges—unless the price of the college is lower than your EFC (in which case you'll likely get no aid and pay full price), or you receive a generous merit scholarship.

If your EFC is low, look for the share of need that the college meets through grants. A higher percentage of need met means the price to you will be closer to your EFC. Some wealthy colleges have "no-loans" policies which means they do not count loans in their financial aid package, and try to make it possible for you to meet your costs without debt.

If your EFC is fairly high and you don't anticipate qualifying for much need-based financial aid, you should consider colleges that are more generous with merit-based aid. If your student has high grades and test scores compared to other applicants for a specific college you may be well positioned to get merit money. For example, if a college's average incoming student has a GPA score of 3.3 and a combined SAT score of 1100, and your student has earned a 3.7 GPA and a 1500 SAT score, you're more likely to get a merit scholarship (assuming the college awards them).

In other words, if your student is high achieving compared to other students at a particular college, applying there could result in your paying less. This means you may be trading prestige for cost—in many cases a trade that families are willing to make in order to provide a debt-free or low-debt future.

Doing the Financial Research to Build Your List

Obviously much of the college search will take place online—and financial research is no exception. Here are the key financial considerations you should track for every college you're considering:

- Published cost of attendance (in-state or out-of-state)
- Forms required (FAFSA, CSS Profile, other)
- Financial aid or scholarship deadline (if different from application deadline)
- Percent of financial need met
- Whether merit aid is available, and the requirements to be considered for it
- How many students typically receive merit aid, and in what average amount
- Average SAT scores or GPA (to see relative strength for merit aid qualification)
- Net price estimates (from the college's net price calculator, or your own research; see below)

As you narrow your list, review colleges' financial aid and admissions websites to learn about the application process and what aid is offered to incoming freshmen. Conduct an internet search for the college's name, plus "merit scholarships" or "financial aid" to zero in on the right pages or other helpful sites.

You should also record the data you find on post-graduation salaries, job placement rates, and graduation rates for each college. These are available from the federal government or from the colleges themselves. It is most useful to compare these metrics with the same metrics from similar colleges, or the colleges on your list, rather than an average across all colleges.

Using College Net Price Calculators

In 2011 the government required that every college and university that grants federal financial aid must share a **net price calculator** on its website in order helps students and parents determine what the actual cost of a given college will be for them.

Although college net price calculators provide more transparency on the true cost of college, like any tool, they're not a one-size-fits-all resource. In fact, they're most effective when used in tandem with other college research strategies to determine best financial fit.

THE PROS OF COLLEGE NET PRICE CALCULATORS

- College net price calculators give better insight into what a college actually costs, not the published costs.
- They can be a great first step for comparing colleges, particularly for narrowing the list of which schools you may be able to afford.
- Net price calculators vary in complexity, but the more thorough ones will allow you to enter a student's test scores and a family's financial assets to get a very personalized estimate of a given college's cost.

THE CONS OF COLLEGE NET PRICE CALCULATORS

- Colleges can be conservative in how they model costs, so the figures presented in the calculators may be higher than the actual net price.
- Net price calculators often only include need-based aid, not merit-based aid—which for some families is a major

contributor to reducing the cost of college.

- Many net price calculators are built on a generic formula and may skimp on or omit specifics.

- There is no standardization across different colleges' net price calculators, so your comparisons may be apples-to-oranges based on the financial/academic information you're asked to submit.

- Net price calculators reflect a moment in time (typically the previous academic year), and may not reflect changes brought about by student enrollments, endowment levels, or other factors.

- College net price calculators can be buried within a college's website and may be hard to track down. (Luckily, the U.S. Department of Education has aggregated many net price calculators on its own site.)

Complete the net price calculator for every college you are interested in, but approach the calculators with a critical eye. How much information they request from you will tell you how

Michael set up a spreadsheet for his daughter, who was a National Merit Semifinalist, to track her applications. They completed the net price calculators for every college on the list. One university's NPC revealed an estimated price of $50,000. But upon more research, they realized this only included financial need-based aid. She would be eligible for an additional $20,000 per year as a result of her National Merit status. They confirmed this with the financial aid department.

personalized the results are, and read the output clearly to understand what costs and aid types are included.

Finance-Related Questions for Your College Visits

Campus visits can occur in the spring of your junior year or in the fall of your senior year, when school is in session and you can see real students and classes. You can also learn a lot during the summer—and you may find you get more time with administrators who can share details about the financial aspects of the student experience.

Shannon Vasconcelos, Director of College Finance and Social Media at Bright Horizons College Coach (and a former financial aid officer), recommends asking the following finance-related questions. You'll notice that many of these questions may not be appropriate for the student who is conducting the tour; consider setting up appointments in advance with the appropriate university staff so that you can get the best information possible.

QUESTIONS FOR THE FINANCIAL AID OFFICE

These are the people who will receive your FAFSA application and, if applicable, your CSS Profile.

- Is my financial aid package likely to change in future years?
- What if my need increases in subsequent years (due to a job loss or sibling going to college, for example)—will my aid package increase or stay the same?
- How much has tuition increased in recent years?
- Can I expect my grant to increase annually as tuition increases?
- What happens to my financial aid if I take longer than four years to graduate?

- Can I borrow student loans to cover the cost of travel or a laptop?
- Do you have suggestions of where to look for a student loan?
- What percent of demonstrated need does the college typically award?
- What percentage of students receive need-based financial aid?

Although your engagement with the admissions office is focused on the application and acceptance process, your relationship with the financial aid office will be ongoing as your aid can be recalculated every year. Approach the financial aid staff with relationship building in mind as you might be working with the same people throughout your student's time in college.

QUESTIONS FOR THE ADMISSIONS OFFICE

Merit scholarships awarded by the college are usually determined by the admissions office. These are also the people who will receive your college application and make acceptance decisions.

- What's the academic profile of a typical scholarship recipient?
- Which merit scholarships are available and is there a process for application?
- Do individual academic departments award scholarships, and if so, what is the application process?
- What are the renewal requirements for your scholarships?
- Do you offer application fee waivers for low income students?
- Do you give college credit for AP tests, and, if so, what score is required?

QUESTIONS FOR THE RESIDENTIAL LIFE OFFICE

Assignments for dormitories, rooms, and first-year roommates are usually handled by the residential life office. Recall that room and board is a significant contributor to the cost of college.

- Is housing guaranteed to freshmen, or is access dependent upon time of deposit?
- If you have to make an early housing deposit, is that deposit refundable if you end up not enrolling?
- Is housing guaranteed to upperclassmen, or do most students move off campus?
- Are first-year students required to live on campus?
- Are there restrictions on which students can live off campus?
- How do off-campus housing costs compare to the dorms?

QUESTIONS FOR THE STUDENT EMPLOYMENT OFFICE

If a financial aid package includes a work-study component, the student employment office will coordinate individual job assignments and process student pay checks.

- What types of jobs on campus are available to first-year students?
- Are on-campus jobs available to students who do not qualify for the need-based Federal Work-Study program?
- How and when can my student apply for a job for freshman year?
- Is there a minimum or maximum number of hours students can work on-campus jobs?

QUESTIONS FOR THE CAREER SERVICES OFFICE

Counselors who staff the college career services office can offer considerable guidance and support in maximizing your financial investment in college. They can also offer valuable data and impressions on how graduates fare financially upon graduation.

- Which companies recruit on your campus?
- What career planning resources do you provide students and alumni?
- Are your career planning efforts focused on graduating seniors, or do you offer help through all four years of college?
- What are the most popular jobs for graduating seniors?
- How many students eventually go on to obtain graduate degrees?

QUESTIONS FOR A SPECIFIC ACADEMIC DEPARTMENT

The admissions office or a department administrator can help you to arrange an advance meeting with a faculty member in a particular area of interest.

- Do you have any departmental scholarships available to students in this major?
- What internship opportunities are available in this field?
- Do students in this major often study abroad, and, if so, where?
- How popular is this particular major?

QUESTIONS FOR CURRENT STUDENTS

Your campus tour guide, who is likely to be a student, is the person best positioned to answer questions about student life on campus. Some colleges can, upon request, also arrange for you to informally meet an individual student or small group of students. Keep your eyes open for friendly students, particularly in the cafeteria or student union, who might be willing to talk with you. They were prospective students in the not-so-distant past!

- Do many students work on campus?
- How easy is it to find a job?
- How do you get around town? Do you need a car, or is there public transportation?
- What do you do for fun?
- How big is Greek life on campus, and what are the costs of joining a fraternity or sorority?
- Do most students travel for spring break?
- How much do season tickets, yoga classes, concerts, or whatever-your-favorite-activity cost around here?

A NOTE ABOUT TEST SCORES

Standardized test scores will be just one part of your application, and may not be a part of it at all: an increasing number of colleges are introducing "test-optional" admissions policies, which means it is up to the student to decide whether or not to submit scores as part of their application. The reality, however, is that many colleges and universities use test scores as a key indicator for whether or not to award merit scholarships to an applicant. In some cases there is an explicit minimum score which will need to be met, and colleges can be very strict about those requirements. Because of this, raising your score even slightly could mean thousands of dollars in additional aid. Studies show that retaking the SAT and ACT can result in significant score improvements—and so we recommend that you consider retaking the test at least once, especially if you see that you could be eligible for more aid with an increased score.

A NOTE ABOUT COLLEGE RANKINGS

Nearly every student and parent knows U.S. News' *Best Colleges*

Rankings. You may have even browsed Times Higher Ed's *U.S. College Rankings*, The Princeton Review's *Best 385 Colleges*, or countless other "top" lists. These news outlets often use similar indicators of academic excellence to produce their rankings, leading to a considerable amount of overlap in their results. However, each ultimately has its own unique approach for measuring a school's value.

Ranking systems can inform your college search somewhat, but most experts will tell you they are very problematic because the metrics and weights they use in their formulas are subjective. Things like how much money professors make, or how many alumni give money to the school, may not correlate with the quality of the education and the outcomes students see.

Second, rankings are not personalized; different people value different things. If you weighted every single factor that was important to you in a college, would Harvard be number one for *you*? Probably not.

Rankings aren't meaningless; they can help you learn about new colleges and do a comparison between them on certain features—but you should always look up the methodology behind the rankings, and make sure the assigned weights reflect your own values about what a good college should offer. Remember that you don't have to agree with a particular ranking, even if it happens to be the most popular or widely used. As conclusive as they may appear to be, ranking systems should ultimately be a fairly unimportant input to your college search.

TAKEAWAYS

- Use the FAFSA4caster to estimate your EFC as you start your college research.
- If your EFC is low, look for colleges that are generous with

need-based aid. If your EFC is high or higher than you'd like, look for colleges that are generous with merit-based aid.

- Public colleges are able to charge lower tuition to in-state students, and out-of-state students pay significantly more. There are some special circumstances in which you could get generous aid as an out-of-state student. Private colleges may be more affordable in some cases because they can offer the most generous financial aid.

- Every college offers a net price calculator; complete these as a step in your research, but be aware that they are not always accurate.

- Use college search tools and college rankings wisely and as a starting point to build your college list, but also consider cost and other factors unique to you.

- Track key financial aid factors as you do your college research and visits, including special deadlines and merit scholarship requirements as well as data on career and graduation outcomes.

CHAPTER FOUR

Senior Year I: Applying

This is the year in which all your savings, research, and planning efforts will begin to pay off by making your student's college application process smoother and—hopefully—more financially rewarding.

At this point, you should have formed some opinions on how much you'll be able to contribute and spend from your savings and income, as well as a range of how much money you'd be comfortable taking in loans. If you're not at that stage, make this your priority as soon as possible. We will share how below.

The first half of senior year is all about filling out applications for financial aid and college admission. Remember that the main two documents for need-based financial aid are the FAFSA and the CSS Profile, which is required at many private universities. Because each form may have different deadlines, it's crucial to stay organized and keep track of what is due when and where.

Almost always, you'll benefit from applying for financial aid earlier. Colleges often budget a certain amount for aid and once it's gone, it's gone.

This chapter will also walk you through how to make your final decisions about where to apply. We'll also give you tips on filling out financial aid forms, and give you an idea of what to expect after you press the button to submit. If you won't qualify for need-based financial aid, we'll review strategies that may result in merit scholarships.

UNDERSTANDING YOUR BUDGET AND SETTING EXPECTATIONS

If you've been doing your research, you've probably collected a lot of data now, of all kinds, about the types of colleges you and your student are considering. You have price estimates, scholarship amounts, your EFC, and the list goes on. But perhaps you've put off some of the more detailed financial discussions while you and your student got your bearings in the process. Here's our advice on how to have those together.

Who Will Be Responsible for College Costs

If you haven't yet done a pen-to-paper calculation of what you could realistically spend on college, now is the time. This doesn't (yet) need to be a detailed monthly budget, but instead a ballpark figure that your student understands. The goal is to get a sense of what's comfortable and what's a stretch as you use more net price calculators and finalize your student's list.

As a reminder, here are the most common components of this contribution calculation:

- *Savings:* money set aside for college, including from your 529 plan. This should not count retirement savings—those are yours and we don't recommend using your retirement nest egg to fund your child's college education.
- *Additional Contributions:* what you and your support

networks (grandparents or others) plan to contribute to the cost of college, above and beyond any savings. This could be $0—but often there is some additional money that you can put towards tuition bills as they come due. For example, if your student won't be living at home you will presumably save on travel and food expenses, and could put that money towards their expenses in college.

- *Student Income:* there are many reasons to work during college, and contributing to the cost of college is top of that list! Even earning a few thousand dollars per year (10 hours per week at the federal minimum wage comes to about $3,500) represents a real reduction in loans you'd need to take otherwise.
- *Additional Scholarships:* if you do have committed or likely scholarships you know about you can include those here also.

Example:

Annual Contributions		
529 Savings Plan	$4,000	The family has saved $16,000 in a 529 plan
Parent Contributions	$5,000	The family estimates they can put aside an additional $5,000 per year for tuition payments

Grandparent Contributions	$3,000	Both sets of grandparents plan to give modest cash gifts to help fund expenses
Student Income	$3,000	The student plans to work every summer
Total Family and Student Contributions	$15,000	If a college costs more than this, the family will need to take on loans

Note: whether or not your student is awarded work-study, once enrolled they will need to search and apply for campus or other jobs each semester. Your student needs to be on top of the job search, do well in order to keep the job, and may need to make some sacrifices if that contribution is critical for you to afford college. If you aren't comfortable with that commitment and risk, you may want to leave it out of your calculation.

As you're understanding what college may realistically cost—and what you can realistically pay for—make sure you look at all four or more years of study. Many students take longer than four years to graduate, so it's worth considering whether you want a cushion for an extra semester or two.

How Much Student (and Parent) Loan Debt is Too Much?

Now is also the time to set some targets for how much you're comfortable taking in loans—as a family. Student debt is actually family

Elizabeth had been saving for her son before he was born and had about $80,000 saved in a 529 plan. She and her husband paid about $25,000 per year for her son to go to private school and planned to contribute the same amount annually to his college tuition payments. They were adamant that they did not want to take out any loans, or to have him take out any loans. They thus decided to focus on colleges that would cost about $40,000-$45,000 per year, taking $20,000 from the 529 plan annually and funding the $25,000 difference from their income.

debt, especially if you'll be co-signing private loans or taking parent loans. The answer to how much student loan debt you and your student can take on, and how much comes from other sources of financing, will be different for every family. Different families will have different risk tolerances based on their financial situation or the student's goals and preferences.

WHAT'S THE LIMIT ON STUDENT BORROWING?

Remember that there are both student and parent loans for college. Federal subsidized or unsubsidized student loans are the first loans your student should take, if you take on any debt. For a dependent student, the total maximum is $31,000 in federal student loans for an undergraduate degree (unless the parents can't qualify for a Parent PLUS loan, in which case it can be higher).

If you need more, you will need to consider one of the following options:

- *Federal PLUS Loans* (Parent PLUS or Graduate PLUS): Direct

PLUS loans are available to parents of undergraduates. They may borrow an amount equivalent to the annual cost of attendance (as determined by the school) minus any other financial aid received. PLUS loans do require a credit check, but approval is much easier than what is generally required for private student loans.

- *Private Loans*: Private student loans are available to both parents and students. Students borrowing privately will almost always need a co-signer, a person who has the income and credit rating required to be approved for the loan, and who agrees to pay the loan if the student cannot. The payment history is also reported on the co-signer's credit report. Private student loans are considered an alternative to PLUS loans because of lower interest rates offered to borrowers or borrowers with co-signers with good credit.

The bottom line: if you have good credit, you could have the option to borrow a lot for college—perhaps up to the full cost—which might be too much debt and hard to pay off. It can be easy to get in over your head at the end of the process, which is why it's important to set your own limits ahead of time. We'll talk about how to choose the right mix of loans later.

MAKING SURE YOU CAN REPAY

One guide to how much to borrow is to look at how much the student will be earning right after college. The benchmark we use: you shouldn't borrow more than your estimated starting salary during your first year out of college. This is a good rule of thumb to ensure that you have enough income to comfortably make your student loan payments over a typical ten-year repayment term. So, if your student anticipates that they'll earn $40,000 in their first

Freda was struggling to make her college decision between her top choice, where she received very little financial assistance, and her state university, where she was awarded a full academic scholarship. Her father was a public school teacher and her mother owned a small business, and were anticipating that their other daughter would be going to college in two years. The parents felt very guilty denying their daughter the college where she would be happiest, and so told her it was her choice. Luckily Freda recognized the risk of signing on to $60,000 in loans–which is what she would have needed to go to the more expensive college. They submitted an appeal to the top choice, but it was rejected–so Freda decided to attend the state university.

entry-level job after graduation, they shouldn't take out more than $40,000 in total student loans.

You can research potential salaries on sites like College Scorecard, Federal Student Aid's Career Search tool, Payscale, or through the college career office.

You can also look at monthly payments and income numbers and aim for 10% of your student's monthly income to go towards loan repayment (this is a slightly more conservative benchmark).

We encourage parents to look at your own goals and life plans and assess how contributing to the education of all of your children will affect your lifestyle and future retirement. When you apply for student loans you'll be approved based on family income, not on what you can safely afford. Use a loan calculator (there are many options available online) to see how much you'll need to pay monthly for different loan amounts. If you can't afford to make the payment now, you more than likely won't be able to afford it when your student finishes college.

Your contributions, plus the loans you could afford, will give you a rough estimate of how much you can responsibly pay for college over the full period. Talk through these numbers with your student and agree on them together. We will discuss affordability in greater detail for making the final college decision, but it's useful to have a number in mind now so that you know your starting budget as you go into the application season.

WHO SHOULD APPLY FOR FINANCIAL AID?

Even if you think you make too much money or believe that your expected financial contribution will be high, you should still plan to fill out the FAFSA and the CSS Profile if applying to colleges that use it. This can be done starting in October of your student's senior year.

"There is no circumstance under which it's not worth applying," says David Sheridan, director of financial aid at Columbia University School of International and Public Affairs. "I've seen people pleasantly surprised by the amount of financial aid they receive. I have seen people who wind up qualifying for more aid than they think they might, so just apply and see what happens."

Here are some other reasons that everyone should complete the FAFSA or CSS Profile:

- All applications for federal student loans require the FAFSA. These are often the best loans to take; even if you don't qualify for need-based aid or subsidized loans, unsubsidized loans are available to every student. Having done the FAFSA keeps your options open.

- If your circumstances change, you may need or qualify for need-based financial aid in the future. In some cases, a college will require you to have filled out the FAFSA before your first year in order to consider you for aid later. One common scenario: if you'll have more than one student in college at the same time in the future, your EFC will be significantly reduced. Additionally, the government may update its eligibility requirements for aid each year—so what didn't qualify this year may make the cut next year.
- Importantly, some colleges and universities require the FAFSA or CSS Profile for consideration for merit aid. Ask the financial aid office if this applies to the schools on your list.
- Some private scholarships also require the FAFSA!

FINALIZING YOUR COLLEGE LIST

You probably have a running list of colleges and perhaps even a spreadsheet where you are tracking your research and keeping tabs on the colleges you are considering. At some point in the fall, you'll stop adding new colleges and start removing the ones your student won't be applying to.

Cost of Applying to College

There are good arguments to apply only to colleges that your student is seriously considering, and also to apply to a balanced list of schools (more on that below). Money is a major factor: applying to college is itself an expense. To add to your budget, below are some of the costs you are likely to incur.

- *SAT and ACT Fees:* It costs money to take the tests and to send score reports to colleges you are applying to.

- *CSS Profile Fees:* Although it's free to file the FAFSA, the CSS Profile costs $25 for the initial application and one college or program report and $16 for each additional report.
- *College Application Fees:* An application fee is the cost a college charges to review a student's application for admittance. The average college application fee costs $43, with the most common cost being $50. However, some colleges charge as much as $100. These fees can add up. The application fees are also generally nonrefundable, regardless if the college admits you or not. Note that a few schools don't charge any application fees and some schools reduce the application fee if you submit early or are applying for financial aid.

FEE WAIVERS IN THE APPLICATION PROCESS

Families can apply for individual fee waivers for each of the itemized costs of applying to colleges, if they need additional financial support. Here are the types of waivers available:

- *SAT and ACT Fee Waivers:* Eligible students can get a fee waiver for the SAT and ACT, which cover registration fees and some number of score reports to send to colleges.
- *CSS Profile Application Fee Waivers:* Reasons for receiving a CSS Profile fee waiver—which covers all application and reporting fees—include receiving the SAT waiver, being an orphan or ward of the court under 24, or meeting family income requirements.
- *College Application Fee Waivers:* You can apply for an application fee waiver at more than 2,000 colleges. However, you will have to apply on a school-by-school basis, and not all schools will accept a waiver.

Balancing Financial Fit

If you've followed along with us, you've done the FAFSA4caster and started filling out net price calculators for some of the schools your student is most interested in. You're also familiar with the type of financial aid you're expecting, and helping your student narrowing their search according to what schools will be generous with students like yours.

Now is the time to make sure that your application list is balanced. In the same way that the list includes academic "reach" schools, some of the schools on the list might be a reach financially. For example, perhaps you've identified a college that awards generous merit awards, but to a small number of students. Even if your student is a strong applicant, there are no guarantees that the offer will be in your range. This could be considered a "financial reach" college. A financial "safety" might be an in-state public university or another college where your student's grades and scores qualify them for significant scholarships that make it affordable.

You'll find as you do your research that some colleges are more noncommittal or vague than others about what they will cost you. Sometimes this is because they don't know themselves—they are leaving their options open to see how their applicant pool shapes up! In other cases, an admissions or financial aid office could be fairly clear with you that a price is the price, and not to expect much of any additional scholarships or discounts. You should pay attention to those signals also. If a college has a very detailed net price calculator and does not award much merit aid, the price you see is probably close to the price you'll pay.

You can also think like an insider and consider what factors the college will be responding to when it sets your financial aid. Harvard isn't hurting for students or tuition dollars—but many colleges in

America are. In the next chapter we'll tell you about "financial aid appeals"—a way that you can ask for more financial aid after receiving your initial acceptance and offer (kind of like a negotiation, though colleges don't like to think about it that way). One of the things that makes appeals most successful is having other offers that you are considering which are lower—especially if those offers are from similar colleges.

Here are some good guidelines:
- Apply to at least one or two private colleges that are tuition dependent, as they tend to have more flexibility on pricing. Factors like a limited endowment or lower selectivity can tip you off about a college's tuition dependency.
- Apply to schools that compete with each other for students—colleges that are similar to each other, in the same region and with the same student profile.
- Make sure you have an in-state public university on your list. Small private colleges are often competing with local public universities for students, so they'll be more willing to come close on pricing for students who are more price sensitive.
- If your admissions safety schools are generous with merit aid, even better since a stronger student is more likely to get scholarship dollars.

Early Decision and Financial Aid

By applying early decision (ED), a student commits to attending the college if admitted and to withdraw any outstanding applications to other schools. Early decision should not be confused with applying early action (EA). Early action acceptance is nonbinding, meaning that students receive an early response, but if accepted do not have to commit to the college until the regular reply date in the spring.

Charles knew that UT-Austin guaranteed full-tuition scholarships to any family making below $65,000 per year (as his family did), and that he'd be automatically admitted based on his class rank. He applied to a variety of private and public universities, and included UT on his list as he knew he could afford the tuition payments there if nothing else worked out.

Early decision is an attractive option because applicants are accepted at higher rates than regular decision applicants. According to a National Association for College Admission Counseling study, 62% of early decision applicants were admitted to schools offering the option, whereas the overall selectivity rate of those schools was 50%.

However, there some big financial-aid-related drawbacks to early decision:

- You may be committing to a more expensive school and giving up the chance to compare financial aid offers from multiple colleges and universities.
- It is very difficult to appeal for more financial aid. An ED offer is generally a "take-it-or-leave-it" situation, and most students that apply ED are committed to going no matter the price. In fact, as a whole, nearly 90% of students admitted ED will go to that college. (ED students tend to come from wealthier backgrounds.) Colleges will expect you to have used their net price calculators before you apply.
- You may receive less merit aid. With ED, the college knows you really want to go there so they might not feel the need

to incentivize you with as much merit money. They may want to save their limited merit money for later in the cycle when it will make a real difference in their yield. ("Yield" means the number of accepted students who actually come to the college.) Contact the school's admissions office if you want to learn more about merit aid in early decision applications.

Note that colleges such as Ivy League universities that do not offer merit aid and base their awards purely on financial need are likely to have well-defined formulas for who gets what aid. Those colleges are more generous with students that demonstrate need via the FAFSA or CSS Profile, and therefore applying ED should not influence the financial aid offer in those cases.

Financial difficulties are an exception to the binding nature of ED—in other words, if you are accepted but really can't afford it, you won't be forced to attend despite financial hardship. In that case you can let the admissions office know and continue applying to other colleges (assuming the deadlines haven't passed). But it is always hard to say no when you have invested so much time and energy, so it is best to be realistic from the start of the process in order to avoid this potential heartache. Do your homework and if you choose the ED route, do so only when you're confident you can afford it.

HOW TO APPLY FOR FINANCIAL AID

Applying for financial aid is a detailed process with many nuances to consider. Completing every step in the process is imperative during the fall and winter of your student's senior year. Decide who is responsible for each form or deadline and consider sharing a paper or electronic calendar with your student to make sure you stay on track during this busy season.

Timelines to Apply for Financial Aid

Timeliness matters, and you should complete the FAFSA, CSS Profile, or any other relevant forms at your earliest convenience after October 1. The sooner you submit, the more money will be available when you're being considered. Getting these things done sooner rather than later can also lessen some anxiety and frees your student to focus on college and scholarship applications.

There are several types of deadlines to keep in mind. The earliest deadline is the deadline you should aim to hit to make sure you're considered for all types of aid.

- *Federal FAFSA Deadlines:* As discussed in Chapter Two, for a given academic year, the U.S. Department of Education usually allows students to submit the FAFSA forms between October of the previous academic year and June of the current academic year. The federal FAFSA deadline is that same June.

- *State FAFSA Deadlines:* Because state budgets allocate money for financial aid, especially for students attending their in-state public colleges, many states have their own FAFSA deadlines. Make sure to check your state's FAFSA deadline early so you don't miss a date that could impact your financial aid package. The U.S. Department of Education has a state FAFSA deadline website, so you can easily find the deadlines that are applicable to you.

- *College FAFSA Deadlines:* Specific colleges will also have their own FAFSA deadline, which may or may not be the same as the federal and state application deadlines. You can usually find this on the admissions or financial aid section of the college's website. Colleges will want to build financial aid packages based on FAFSA results, meaning that you need to complete the FAFSA before the college's deadline in order to be considered for financial aid.

- *CSS Profile Deadlines:* If your student is applying to private colleges that require you to fill out the CSS Profile for financial aid consideration, each college will have a specific deadline for that form as well. Again, inquire with the school's financial aid office at the time of applying for admission so you know everything that's required.

- *Merit Scholarship Deadlines:* As with the FAFSA and CSS Profile above, colleges can also set earlier application deadlines for those that wish to be considered for merit scholarships—so pay attention to those.

Documents You'll Need

Make sure that you have all of the necessary documents ready by the time that you and your student sit down to fill out your paperwork. Below is a breakdown of what forms you will need to tackle the FAFSA and/or CSS Profile.

For both the FAFSA and the CSS Profile:

- Your Social Security Number (or, your Alien Registration Number if you are not a U.S. citizen)

- Your federal income tax returns, W2s, and other records of money earned. These documents must contain the records of the current year's and last year's income as well as taxes owed and paid

- Bank statements and records of investments (if any exist)

- Records of untaxed income (if any exists)

For the FAFSA:

- An FSA ID to sign electronically (you can obtain this ID by registering on the Federal Student Aid website)

For the CSS Profile:

- A College Board account (if your student has taken the SAT, PSAT, or any AP Credit classes, they may already have one)
- Your mortgage information and home equity value
- Information regarding ownership of small businesses and other assets

What Happens After You Submit the FAFSA?

Within three to five business days of filing the FAFSA, you will receive your Student Aid Report (SAR) via email or mail. At that point, you will be able to see any problems or issues that may need to be resolved, along with detailed instructions on how to resolve them.

Once you receive your SAR, make sure to review it thoroughly, verifying that all of the information is correct. The SAR will show the EFC that will be sent to the colleges and universities that your student chose when filling out the FAFSA.

In order to correct any information on your FAFSA, simply go back to the FAFSA homepage and edit your information. Then, as before, you will receive a newly updated SAR report via email within three to five days.

After submitting corrections or additional information that may inevitably change your financial profile, it's important to check in again with the colleges you selected to ensure that they don't need additional information on their end to reassess their financial aid decision and your aid package.

For CSS Profile colleges, you'll need to work directly with each admissions or financial aid office to make corrections according to their process.

APPLY!

And then, you apply! You should know what you need to do to submit applications to the colleges on your list and if there are any additional steps you need to do to be considered for financial aid. There's a bit of a waiting period between now and what happens in the next chapter, when we'll talk about what to do when you start to get your admissions decisions back.

TAKEAWAYS

- Set boundaries as a family about how much you want to spend on college, who will pay what, and whether you are willing to take loans—and, if so, how much debt you are willing to take on.
- Build a balanced list that includes at least a few colleges that you know will be affordable for you as well as colleges whose offers can help you appeal for more financial aid.
- If your student has high grades and test scores compared to the applicant pool for a specific college, you may be well positioned to attract merit scholarships.
- Although applying early decision increases your chances of acceptance, you'll forgo the ability to compare multiple financial aid offers and you may be less likely to receive merit aid.
- Apply for financial aid even if you think you make too much money to qualify.
- Check the FAFSA federal, state, and specific college deadlines, and the CSS Profile deadlines, if applicable.
- Applying earlier for financial aid may increase your aid package.

CHAPTER FIVE

Senior Year II: Deciding

R egular decision college acceptance letters are mailed in the spring. This is also when you receive financial aid letters—usually sent around the same time as or shortly after the acceptance letters. Each financial aid package includes a combination of grants or scholarships, work-study, and loans.

As you compare and make your decision about where to enroll, keep in mind that the school that offers the most generous financial aid may not be the least expensive school to attend if there is a large gap between the amount offered and your net cost. By a similar calculation, the school that offers the least amount of aid may not be the most expensive school to attend if the school's sticker price is relatively low, if your student lives at home, or if the school's geographic location offers relatively inexpensive room and board possibilities.

The offers may also differ in the amount of money you are asked to borrow. After receiving financial aid offers, some families choose the college that will have the lowest net cost while other families factor financial aid into other considerations.

This chapter will give you helpful guidelines for comparing, deciding, and accepting financial aid as well as advice on how you might appeal your financial aid offer. When making this important decision, you will want to consider the various types of loans—including their comparative advantages and disadvantages as well as the requirements for keeping and spending a merit scholarship. You'll also want to consider possible effects on your financial aid if grandparents or other relatives will contribute money.

UNDERSTANDING YOUR COSTS

Once you receive financial aid package info, what it will cost you to attend a given college is no longer hypothetical! You will want to compare those costs, apples to apples, and compare them to your desired budget.

Reading Your Financial Aid Letters

Financial aid letters are notorious for being confusing, occasionally misleading, and non-standardized—in other words, every college does things a little differently. A recent study from the New America Foundation, *Decoding the Cost of College*, analyzed 11,000 aid letters. Researchers found that they used vague terms and definitions and often omitted cost information or failed to calculate what the student would actually need to pay.

Having followed along with us in the book, you should have a good foundation for interpreting your letter—but we'd urge you to contact the university if you have any questions or points of confusion as you do so. Here are the steps to take to create an apples-to-apples cost comparison.

Calculating Your Actual Net Price

We recommend you create a spreadsheet to compare each college side by side.

First, find the full published cost of attendance. Note that some schools may not give costs to you in the letter; others might omit personal expenses from the calculation, and some will enumerate everything. Attempt to find figures for every cost category, including fees.

Then, look for the types of aid you are being offered. Start with "free money," the money that you don't have to repay (i.e. loans) or work for (i.e. work-study). This kind of aid is almost always called "grants" or "scholarships," and there may be multiple different lines in your letter. Add them all up.

Many colleges will include loans and work-study in their financial aid letter as those are supports that can help you cover the cost. Leave those out for now as they are not free money.

Example:

University Of Your State	
College Costs (Tuition, Fees, Room and Board)	$25,000
(-) Scholarships and Grants	-$10,000
(=) Amount Paid to College	+$15,000
(+) Additional Living Expenses (Travel, Clothing, Books, etc.)	+$5,000
Total Required (Your Cost)	$20,000

This is your actual cost for attending this college. Recall that this amount is what you are responsible for and will need to pay somehow: either with loans, cash, or by working.

Think Ahead

College is not just one year; it's usually at least four to get a bachelor's degree, and every year has tuition and costs associated. Consider inflation and tuition increases. The school tuition can change and is likely to, though some schools freeze tuition or commit to making up the difference in financial aid. Check your financial aid package or ask the college's financial aid office what their policy is.

Make sure to look at all four years, and to know what it will take to maintain your scholarships and grants. Most financial aid letters with a need-based aid component have a clause stating that awards are contingent on further verification (even if you haven't received that request yet). Additionally, need-based aid awarded in future years is likely to require reverification. So, if there's anything that has changed in your financial situation since completing the FAFSA, you'll want to make sure you think about the impact on your student's financial aid awards.

Merit scholarships often require showing satisfactory academic progress by maintaining a certain GPA and number of credit hours.

Calculating Your Gap

Recall your contribution amount from Chapter Four, which was the amount you thought you could pay for college before accounting for any loans.

If awarded work-study, you can update your calculation to reflect that income for that college. Keep in mind that, much like working in the adult world, this money isn't free money. Being awarded federal work-study indicates that there are designated funds for your student to earn through a campus job. This is not a 100% guarantee, though, as the available work-study jobs might not fit their schedule, skills, or interests.

Your net price, minus your contributions, is the gap that you would need to account for if your student attends that college.

Example:

University Of Your State	
Total Required	$20,000
(-) Family and Student Contributions	-$15,000
(=) Gap	$5,000

You should still leave loans out while you focus on whether you can close the gap with a financial aid appeal.

FINANCIAL AID APPEALS

Now you have a sense of the relative cost of each college option, and of the gap you have between your contributions and that cost. The next thing to consider is whether you would like to appeal your financial aid award, as this can change the financial picture significantly for a college's cost.

An "appeal" means a communication to ask for more money from a school so that college costs less.

Who Can Appeal

Any family who has received an insufficient offer of financial aid is eligible to appeal—and as a general rule, it never hurts to ask. But as with any request, it's important to have a clear reason and justification for why the extra dollars will be meaningful to your decision.

Appeals are most often successful when a significant change

affecting the student's financial situation, such as the death of a parent, serious illness, job or income loss, or divorce has occurred. In those cases the college is often able to "update" the student's EFC in order to recalculate aid.

Merit-based appeals are possible as well. If you received more scholarships at another college, that can be a fair reason for an appeal.

The reason a college would grant an appeal is to help you say yes to them! So appeals always work best if you can say with honesty that a college is your top choice or one of your top choices and that you'd happily attend if they can help you make it work financially. If you've demonstrated your interest by being engaged with events, talking to alumni or students, visiting the campus, or in other ways, that will help.

You should also consider the type of college as you develop your appeal strategy:

- Public institutions tend to have less flexibility. State oversight of the institution's practices means they may be more concerned than a private institution about consistency across students. Large public universities have fewer resources to manage an in-depth appeal process compared to a small school, where one-on-one conversations are easy to come by. State schools also tend to be less generous with out-of-state students as they have a higher priority to meet the financial needs of in-state students.

- Very selective institutions who do not award merit aid have comprehensive and detailed formulas to evaluate your financial need. Most use the CSS Profile and have a lot of detail on your finances already. Therefore, it's fairly unlikely you'll be able to persuade them that their initial award is mistaken—unless there have been significant changes since you filled out the FAFSA or CSS Profile, or unless there is something about your situation that those forms didn't capture. Their acceptance rates are very low, so they have lots of other students waiting for the chance to attend if your student doesn't.

- Selective institutions who do award merit aid are likely to be very focused on their yield, and on attracting high achieving students who can help their rankings. For these schools, competitive offers from schools that are similar to them can go far.

- Smaller private colleges are more dependent on every seat being filled. We've found that those schools are most likely to work with you on an appeal if the initial offer is not viable for your situation.

When and How to Appeal

Generally speaking, you can begin to prepare your appeal as soon as your financial aid offer letter arrives. A school may not have a specific deadline by which appeals must be submitted, but because they have a limited amount of financial aid dollars to distribute each year the earliest-received appeals have a greater chance of approval. Students who experience a significant change in financial circumstances at any time prior to the start of or during the school year should not hesitate to appeal for additional financial aid at the time when the adverse change occurs.

The process differs for every school. In addition, the types of documentation required for an appeal differ based on the underlying reason(s) for the appeal. Many schools, especially larger colleges and universities, publish information online regarding their appeals processes. In addition, don't hesitate to call the financial aid or admissions office directly.

For your appeal to be successful, it's important to comply with the school's specific procedures for evaluating appeals, including providing all the necessary documents and information in the formats requested.

Depending on the nature of your appeal, you may be asked to provide:

- Documentation of a change in financial circumstances, perhaps related to death of a family member, serious illness, loss of a job or other income, or divorce or separation
- Documentation demonstrating unmet financial need, perhaps in the form of a family budget
- Documentation of academic progress or achievement, such as letters of recommendation, school transcripts, or coursework certificates
- Documentation of a more attractive financial aid package offered by another school

After you prepare the documentation, write a letter that summarizes why you're submitting an appeal and how much additional aid you are requesting. Be specific—calculate your family's unmet financial need to determine exactly how much more support you require.

Unless your school specifically instructs otherwise, we recommend calling the financial aid office to initiate the appeal process. Your goal, to the extent that it is feasible for you, should be to arrange a call or an in-person meeting with a financial aid officer.

During the meeting you want to clearly state your goals and the rationale for your appeal. Speak assertively but non-confrontationally. Remember that you have requested a reconsideration. You are not there to strike a special deal or negotiate in the traditional sense of the word. You're better positioned if you treat the financial aid officer as a partner and potential advocate, rather than as an adversary.

You are unlikely to receive a decision on your appeal during the first meeting, but before the meeting is concluded, make sure to ask the administrator about the next steps in the process. You'll want to know exactly how and when to follow up with the financial aid officer.

Penny had used net price calculators and saw that her son Martin's top choice private university in Ohio was potentially about $10,000 too expensive. Her EFC was around $30,000 and she knew she needed to get merit aid as well as financial need-based aid in order to afford a private college. She added a similar private college to the list, where her son was also a competitive applicant. Her thought process was that this way she'd have prices from two similar colleges, both of which award merit scholarships, to compare. When his financial aid letters arrived there was a difference of about $5,000 between them. Upon sending an appeal letter they were awarded $6,000 additional dollars from the top choice college. In a twist, the second college also increased their initial grant, by $5,000, after Martin visited the financial aid office and asked in person about the possibility of receiving more money. For a variety of reasons, not all financial, the "second choice" became the top choice—and the family decided that Martin would go there!

We recommend you follow up with your request in writing if you have not sent it prior to your meeting—typically via email is fine. Send it to a person rather than "Financial Aid Office" if you can.

If your financial aid appeal is approved, then you will receive a new offer that includes more or additional forms of financial assistance.

FILLING YOUR GAP

Once you've gone through appeals processes and done your math, you now know how much each school will cost you, and how those costs might change over the course of your student's studies. Let's return to your gap, as funding that gap is the last step in figuring out how you'll pay for college.

Is It Worth Stretching For?

This is where it "gets real," so to speak, and when you might start to ask, *"Is this really worth it?"*

Particularly when weighing schools with significantly different costs, many families aren't sure how to quantify the value of one school over another. Will that extra $7,000 per year be worth it for that private school? What about an extra $15,000 per year? Particularly if loans are involved, the cost differences over four years, plus any interest, can add up quickly.

There's no perfect formula for this decision. Your prior thinking about college ROI should impact what you are willing to do to fill your gap.

Perhaps you're considering a financial-stretch college which you think would be much better for your student—that's kind of a "high risk, high return" situation since you're putting more of your money on the line for something that could turn out to be really worth it. Or maybe you're feeling pinched and want to be more conservative with this decision, minimizing your risk by taking only federal student loans and no private or parent loans (and paying less out of pocket).

Recall the following risk-reducers, which we laid out in the first section of the book on college costs and ROI:

First, ensure your student will feel happy and well-supported by the college in order to graduate, and to graduate on time. There is no one-size-fits all formula to make sure your student graduates and graduates on time, but they can set themselves up for success by preparing academically: building good study skills in high school, and perhaps taking a college course or two if it's offered so that they feel ready for that level of work. It's also important to evaluate the advising and student support available at the colleges you consider. A college's published graduation rate is not a predictor of whether your student will graduate, but it can be a sign of how well the college supports students. You can also speak with alumni and current students to learn about this.

Second, ensure the college you choose has strong career outcomes, career services, and career opportunities.

Third, consider your student's interests and anticipated major. It's ok if they aren't sure or are interested in a less lucrative path. Clearly a student's aptitude for and interest in the topic will dictate their academic success, engagement in school, and happiness in whatever career is chosen—but if they are choosing a major or career path that leads to lower average incomes, you might want to consider optimizing for lower price and debt to reduce your risk. Think ahead to the financial implications of graduate school also.

Beware stretching beyond the benchmarks we've discussed

and the lines you have drawn in past planning exercises—especially those involving debt. Many families get to the end of the process and find it very hard to turn down a dream college, even when it is really out of range. But this decision will follow you for many years!

What Loans to Take

In general, our recommendation is to first take subsidized student federal loans, then unsubsidized student federal loans, and then loans from your state or college if available. Federal student loans have better repayment terms, low interest rates, easy approval, and affordable loan limits. They also offer more protective mechanisms: if your student is having trouble making the loan payments, there are income-based repayment programs (which allow you to reduce your payments based on your income), loan forgiveness programs, and financial hardship provisions such as deferment and forbearance (which allow you to temporarily stop or reduce payments).

If your family plans to take more debt than is available with federal student loans, you'll have to choose between private loans (for students or for parents) and federal parent loans (Parent PLUS loans).

Compared to private loans, Parent PLUS loans are easier to get. The government has minimal standards for adverse history that could cause denial, but those standards are more lenient than for private loans. You can also borrow as much as you need up to the school's cost, as opposed to private loans which will set limits based on your scores and income.

However, if you have good credit and are willing to give up the federal loan protections that come with Parent PLUS, private loans can sometimes offer lower interest rates and initiation fees.

Private loans can be issued to the student or the parent directly—but in either case the parent is likely to be involved, as the vast majority of private student loans require a co-signer. Some lenders provide for "co-signer release," meaning that the co-signer can be taken off the loan after certain requirements are met (for instance, on-time payments for a given period).

If you do decide to take private loans, applications will happen over the summer and you should apply to multiple lenders to compare their rates and terms. The most important things to compare will be the interest rates (lower is better!) and the fees.

When doing your cost comparisons, look at how long it will take to repay your loans, and how much you will pay in interest and fees, in addition to just the monthly payment.

Here's a summary of the key terms and benefits of each type of loan:

	Federal Student Loans	Federal Parent Loans	Private Loans
Payments Begin	Payments begin when the student graduates, leaves school, or changes their status to less than half-time		Depends on loan terms
Interest Rates	Fixed	Fixed (and different than student loans)	Depends on the borrower and loan terms

Consolidation And Refinancing	Federal Direct Consolidation Loans are available to combine multiple loans into one (potentially with lower monthly payments and longer repayment time)		Not eligible for federal consolidation but you can refinance in the private sector
Credit Check Required	No	Yes, though standards are generous	Yes, and co-signer often required
Repayment Plans	Several options are available including income-based repayment, which recalculates your monthly payment based on your income		Depends on loan terms
Loan Forgiveness	Under the Public Service Loan Forgiveness (PSLF) program, student loan balance can be forgiven after 10 years of on-time payments while working in public service		Unlikely

Adapted from Federal Student Aid

When doing your cost comparisons, look at how long it will take to repay your loans, and how much you will pay in interest and fees, in addition to just the monthly payment.

Other Ways to Fill the Gap

Other sources of cash may provide additional support but could have tax implications. You should consult an accountant or financial advisor to understand if any of these options are right for you.

Many families rely on financial help from grandparents or other relatives. Substantial cash gifts have potential penalties due to gift-tax limits and the requirement to report it as student income on the FASFSA. Relatives can elect to write a check directly to the student's college or university to cover tuition. As long as the check is paid directly to the school, they won't incur a gift tax. However, it will still get reported on the FAFSA as untaxed income—which will impact financial aid awards and may result in less need-based money the following year.

Other families consider home equity loans or home equity lines of credit, or use their retirement savings to pay for students' college by withdrawing early or taking out a loan on their 401(k). These alternatives offer none of the protections provided to borrowers by the U.S. Department of Education for federal student or parent loans and could also jeopardize the financial stability of the family, so proceed with caution and seek experienced advice.

Creating New Options

If you still can't map out how exactly you'll pay for all four (or more) years of college, this should be a big warning sign. "We'll figure it out" is not a plan! While it's very difficult to acknowledge it, if you've reached this point and feel nervous about the financial commitment, you should pause to consider some new options. Postponing a year to reapply can allow you to add new colleges to your list that will be more affordable. You can also consider community college. Pursuing courses at a local two-year institution

Ashley was choosing between her state public university and an expensive private school in New York City. She was lucky enough to have a full tuition scholarship from the private college due to a very strong academic record, but would still have to cover her living costs, which would be high (about $24,000 per year). Her local university had also given her a small scholarship, and would cost around $19,000 per year. While she was not eligible for any additional aid from the private university, the family decided that the opportunity to study in New York was not one to turn down given the strong career outcomes that graduates from the private university had. Ashley ended up taking federal loans to cover the difference.

can be a very affordable way to get a start on college—and if your student transfers to a four-year institution, their degree will be the same one you'd get as if you'd started there!

Make your full plan for how you are going to fill your gap, including who will take what amount in loans, before you give the colleges your decision.

SIGNING ON THE DOTTED LINE

May 1 is sometimes called "decision day" because it's the deadline for telling the college that you're enrolling. If you miss the deadline, you may lose your spot—but don't feel pressured to decide before May 1 if you are still working out what's right for you. Many colleges continue to enroll students well after May 1, and recent changes in the rules that govern admissions practices may make this deadline even less meaningful in the future.

At the end of the day you'll be weighing a lot of factors in this decision—some rational, some emotional, some yours, and some your student's. Only you can decide what's worth it and what's not for your family. The most important thing is to align with your student on why and what assumptions you're making, whether financial (*we can make this work if you work a job through school, or if you live off campus*) or intangible (*I think I'll be more likely to thrive at this college*).

After Accepting Your Admissions Offer
Once you do decide, here are the steps to take.

ACCEPTING AND RECEIVING YOUR AID
Instructions for accepting and rejecting aid will be included within your financial aid package. Once you have reviewed your aid options and are ready to decide, follow the provided instructions for completion. It's not an all-or-nothing offer—so you can pick and choose the aid you accept.

SEND IN YOUR DEPOSIT
You will be required to send along a tuition deposit with your acceptance decision confirmation. This is a relatively small amount—usually in the hundreds of dollars—that will hold your spot. It basically tells the school that you are serious about moving forward and attending. After your deposit is applied to your total bill, you will receive an updated bill with the remaining balance.

PLAN YOUR TUITION PAYMENTS
After sending in your tuition deposit, you will receive a tuition bill

that has considered all the scholarships, work-study, and loans that you have accepted to calculate what you owe for the academic year. Although you are usually expected to pay for each term in one or two rather large payments, the bursar's office may offer additional plans that are more flexible, for example, smaller monthly payments.

COMPLETE LOAN PAPERWORK

Student loans require that you fill out the necessary loan paperwork, including promissory notes, entrance interviews, and other agreements. Make sure to carefully read your loan paperwork before signing.

RECEIVING YOUR AID

Your school is required to make grant and loan payments at least twice a year, and often will do so once a term (semester, quarter, trimester).

Your student's college will first use your grant and loan money to cover the semester's tuition, fees, and room and board (if they live on campus). Any money left over will be provided to you for other school expenses. You will likely get to choose how you receive that money.

In the case of federal loans, if a loan payment is automatically disbursed and you no longer need that money, you have 120 days to cancel it for no fee and with no interest charged.

If your student is on work-study, their school job is required to pay them at least once a month. They will be paid like any other job: by check, direct deposit, or cash for the hours worked. They'll be expected (but not required) to use these earnings toward school-related needs. Some schools will allow them to put all or some of their earnings directly back into the school to cover tuition or fees.

TAKEAWAYS

- Consider the ROI of a college, comparing its cost with expected earnings. You should also consider factors such as plans for graduate school when assessing how much you are willing to pay and how much debt you can take on.
- You can appeal your financial aid offer; it pays to strategize and prepare the right message in order to maximize your chances of success.
- When accepting your financial aid package, accept free money first, work-study opportunities second, and then loans in the smallest amount you can afford
- Both students and parents can take on loans to pay for college. For students, federal loans tend to offer more favorable terms than private loans. Private student loans almost always require a co-signer. For parents, Parent PLUS loans from the government are easier to obtain than private loans but tend to have higher interest rates.
- If grandparents or other relatives contribute there may be financial aid and tax implications.

CHAPTER SIX

During College:
Staying on Track

D uring college, families can and should continue the conversations about money—ensuring that your college costs don't increase beyond what you'd planned for in the years leading up to it. Resubmitting the FAFSA and CSS Profile each year, and fulfilling requirements for merit scholarships are necessary for keeping financial aid throughout the four years of college.

Students who become increasingly independent in their lives and studies can also become more independent financially by taking responsibility for daily spending habits, creating a budget, and working to earn money from a job. This chapter walks through the major fixed and variable expenses that students incur in college, which can inform a detailed personal budget for your student. We also describe circumstances that might affect continuing financial aid during college, such as receiving merit scholarships or a sibling's enrollment.

Although this is by no means a comprehensive overview of managing finances in college, it should help you avoid some of the pitfalls that can lead to higher debt than needed and more difficulties paying off your educational expenses.

KEEPING YOUR FINANCIAL AID

Many things can change during four or more years of college. Your student can be awarded additional scholarship money, a sibling may enter or leave college, and your income may rise or fall. Anticipate these changes so you're prepared for the impact on your financial aid.

Scholarship Displacement

If your student is awarded a private scholarship, then, in accordance with federal law, you must report it to your school. Scholarship displacement is when a school reduces the amount of financial aid that is available to you based on the value of the private scholarships that a student has received.

Scholarship displacement policies are established individually by each school and vary widely. They're implemented regardless of whether or not you obtained the scholarship in effort to cover a budget shortfall. If you're hoping to fill a gap between what you can pay and what the college will charge you, scholarship displacement could actually mean the gap is increased.

It's difficult to completely avoid scholarship displacement, although not impossible. If you might be in the position where your aid is disrupted because of an outside scholarship, contact your financial aid office to see what your options are.

Multiple Children in College

If the number of children in college at a time changes, it may affect your financial aid eligibility and how much total aid you receive. If another child enters college, your EFC is likely to go down significantly, and you may get more aid. If a child graduates college, your EFC for the younger child could go up significantly.

Changes in Finances
If a single parent gets married, or someone's salary increases due to a raise or job change, the increased income of the household will be reflected in your FAFSA and can affect your financial aid. Similarly, if a grandparent or other relative gives cash or pays tuition on your behalf, this is counted as untaxed student income and could impact your aid negatively for future years.

Note that since the FAFSA is a year behind, the impact of these changes will be less or none if they happen later in the student's college studies.

Eligibility for Scholarships
As mentioned in Chapter Five, your scholarships may come with requirements about maintaining a certain GPA or course load; they may also be tied to a particular department, major, or activity. Keep those top of mind and be prepared accordingly.

BUDGETING FOR COLLEGE
Your calculations in the research and decision process may have relied on the estimated cost of attendance provided by the university. The loans you are given also assumed that you need that amount of money to subsist during the year. But of course every student will have different expenses—and there may be opportunities to spend less than that cost of attendance, meaning you take less debt and pay it all off sooner after college.

College is an opportunity to practice sound financial habits by creating a budget, spending responsibly, learning to save, and, of course, earn money. As you enter the summer and beyond, it's wise to make a more detailed budget that you and your student share.

Fixed Expenses

An important part of your budget is a category called fixed expenses. These are all of your recurring bills and costs that are mandatory and stay relatively consistent each month.

Some call this category "survival needs." Fixed expenses have to be paid by an individual each month regardless of the change in use.

If you're putting together a comprehensive college budget, fixed expenses should include tuition, fees, and on-campus housing (if your student chooses to live on campus). Whether your student stays on campus each weekend, chooses to travel, or go home, housing costs will remain the same.

If your student will be living off-campus, you'll need to budget for rent and utilities. We suggest researching average prices specific to the area in which the school is located. Don't forget to leave space for internet in your budget; an average price for internet is $65 per month. Multiply monthly payments by nine months to figure out the full school-year budget.

To figure out what else should go in this category, look at your bank statements for the last three to four months and find recurring expenses. Then, evaluate if you foresee having those costs moving forward. If you do, it's a clear indication that they should be included in your budget as fixed expenses You'll want to consider recurring expenses such as your cell phone and health insurance.

Variable Expenses

Variable expenses change based on your use or volume. You can easily adjust variable expenses as a category based on the lifestyle choices that you. The good news is that these are expenses you can reduce fairly easily by cutting down on frequency or volume of certain activities. But it is also an area of the budget where students tend to overspend. It is important to be mindful of variable expenses and to track spending closely to make sure you don't go above the allocated amounts. This maintenance and attention will make sure the budget as a whole stays on track.

Variable expenses for college students include restaurant meals, clothing, laundry, travel, and textbooks.

Commonly Overlooked Expenses

The more nuanced your budget, the better prepared both you and your student will be for the costs of college.

CLOTHING

Your student may attend college in a climate that requires different clothing than they have—for example, winter gear for a student from Florida who is going to college in Massachusetts. You will also want to budget for professional attire for interviews and jobs while in college.

FOOD

"Food" is always a highly contested line-item on a college student's budget. Some students consider food a fixed expense because they have to purchase a meal plan and its cost doesn't change month to month—in other words, whether they choose to eat in the cafeteria or not, they'll still be charged that semester fee if the meal plan is mandatory. Food can also be considered a fixed expense because it's a "survival need." Most students put groceries in their fixed expense category.

On the flip side, many students consider food a variable expense. If you're talking about going out to eat at restaurants, getting take-out, or doing an occasional run to a café, food can be considered a variable expense. And although you need to eat in order to survive, going out to dinner with your friends is not necessarily a matter of survival: it's just something fun to do. It's perfectly fine to have food-related line items in both fixed and variable expense categories.

TEXTBOOKS AND COURSE SUPPLIES
Common estimates put textbooks and course materials at ~$1,200 per academic year or more. In addition to books, certain classes could also have materials fees such as lab fees. There are ways to save some decent money on this budget item, including renting, borrowing, sharing, or buying used textbooks.

TRAVEL AND TRANSPORTATION
Travel and transportation are technically two different budget line items to consider when budgeting for college.

Transportation pertains to public-transit passes and ride-hailing services as well as the costs of having a car on campus. Transportation costs will be higher if your student will be commuting to and from off-campus housing or employment, or if the campus is large enough to require a car or public transportation to get around.

Travel pertains to the cost of traveling between school and home. Travel costs will vary depending on how frequently your student comes home and the distance from school to home. Travel may also entail visiting friends at other colleges or vacation destinations for spring break. Consider your own travel too, as you may want to visit your student a couple of times per year!

ACTIVITIES
If your student decides to "Go Greek" during college by joining a fraternity or sorority, encourage them to take careful consideration of the associated costs and weigh the options. Membership dues and other fees can range from several hundred to thousands of dollars. Plus, social events are not generally covered by membership dues and will sometimes require additional spending. The same can apply to other extracurricular activities and clubs.

WORKING DURING COLLEGE
According to the National Center for Education Statistics, approximately 70% of undergraduates work while in college. From a financial perspective, every dollar earned is a dollar not borrowed or spent from savings. And contributing to the cost of college teaches important lessons that benefit life after graduation, such as time management, responsibility, and working with others. A job related to a student's studies can also be a huge advantage after graduation.

In terms of financial aid, a student can make up to a particular amount of non-work-study taxable or untaxable income before it is counted as income and used in calculating your financial aid package for the following year. The student income allowance is $6,660 for 2019-2020.

Work-Study
A work-study job enables students to earn a pre-set amount of money each semester that can be used to help pay for education

and living expenses. Work-study jobs are typically on campus and often involve helping out at the library, dining hall, or some other campus operations department. After the first year, when students choose a major and develop recognizable interest areas, some work-study jobs, such as becoming a research assistant for a faculty doing research, can be more closely tied to career development.

These jobs are usually between six and 12 hours per week, which means students can predict exactly how much money they'll earn and how many hours they'll be able to devote to schoolwork.

Participants earn at least the federal minimum wage, but they may earn more depending on the skill set required for their job. According to the *2015-16 National Postsecondary Student Aid Study* by the National Center for Education Statistics, 5.2% of undergraduate students received aid through work-study programs during the 2015-16 academic year. They earned an average of $2,400.

Note that money earned through work-study is meant to be allocated toward living expenses—it does not get applied directly to tuition. Although work-study income is considered taxable and will need to be claimed during tax time with the IRS, it is not listed as income on the FAFSA. Work-study income also doesn't reduce aid eligibility for the following year.

Part-Time Jobs

Earning money from a part-time job is also an option, especially if your student isn't eligible for a work-study position. There are many advantages to a "regular" job. They may pay more than minimum wage, offer more hours, or be more in line with areas of interest. Some students may parlay a part-time job during the academic year into a full-time job during the summer months.

Disadvantages may include the cost and time of commuting

and an employer who is less flexible to an academic schedule. Also, there may be more competition for jobs that are not part of a school's work-study program.

Internships

Internships enable students to acquire work experience applicable to a future career. Internships are either paid or unpaid. Although a paid internship is clearly advantageous, unpaid internships may offer college credits (which have monetary value, since you would have had to pay tuition for those!). They can also be opportunities for students to build connections which will later help them in their job search as many graduates get their first jobs after college from former internship sites or internship site contacts.

A 2015 report, *Learning by Earning*, by Georgetown University's Center for Education and the Workforce, reported the starting annual salary for college graduates who completed a paid internship was higher than for those who did not.

Coops

Cooperative education programs, or "coops", vary from school to school. Usually, when a student participates in a coop, they stop taking classes to gain on-the-job experience and work full time.

Coops are usually paid, and give students more extensive work experience, which can provide an advantage when applying for jobs post-college. Depending on the college, you may not be charged for tuition while participating in the coop, which means earning money, gaining work experience and a break in tuition payments. The downside is that coop programs may extend time until graduation.

TAKEAWAYS

- College is an opportunity for your student to develop a budget for managing their expenses and developing personal finance skills.
- Tuition and room and board will be the largest fixed expenses for your student; variable expenses can range widely depending on personal preference and constraints.
- Keep tabs on your financial aid year to year by completing the FAFSA or CSS Profile annually and anticipating large changes due to multiple children in college or income fluctuations.
- Students can earn income during college through work-study jobs, part-time jobs, coop programs, summer employment, and internships. All have financial benefits and can also be helpful for developing your student's long-term career interests and job prospects.

Conclusion

We hope that after reading this book you feel prepared to tackle the college process with confidence that you and your family can be better off after sending your student to college.

In Chapter One you learned that whatever you can save for college throughout your student's life will have great consequences for your family. Every dollar you set aside will compound if invested—meaning you'll need to come up with less or borrow less when it comes time to pay for college. And because borrowed dollars incur interest, those savings could multiply even more.

To illustrate: you could expect a dollar saved at a child's birth to be worth $3 or more when they go to college. That's $3 you won't have to borrow in loans, which would ultimately cost you $5 or more with interest over a typical repayment period. In other words, that one dollar of savings is actually worth five of debt!

In Chapters Two and Three you learned that there are two main ways that the colleges will discount their published costs for your student, resulting in a much lower net price. The first is with financial need-based aid, which will largely be driven by the financial information you provide on the FAFSA or CSS Profile. You can use the government's FAFSA4caster tool to estimate your EFC and the colleges' net price calculators to get an early sense for how much need-based aid you are likely to receive. The second way to lower your costs is with merit-based scholarships. There is always a college that will want your student and make it financially attractive for them to attend if you are strategic about the college list you build.

In Chapters Four and Five you learned that the early bird gets the worm. Make sure you complete your FAFSA shortly after October 1 of your student's senior year, and then finalize your applications. Remember that after you are accepted, you will receive a financial aid letter with your actual costs. You can often attempt to get more by making a formal request to the college's financial aid or admissions office, called a financial aid appeal. If you applied to financial safety schools and similar colleges to your targets, you will most likely be able to get one or more colleges to give you a little more financial aid.

When making your final decision, consider not only the cost of the college but also the ROI. What will the student get out of college, including job prospects and earnings over the course of their career? A "cheap" school isn't necessarily the best approach—nor is simply going to the highest ranked selective college. Compare the college's actual costs and the amount of debt you will need to take to pay for it with your student's expected first year salary. If you are going to stretch, make sure it is worth it for your family. Note that the student's major and career path will have a big impact on earnings, and thus should be considered when choosing where to attend and how much debt you will be able to afford.

If you need to take out debt, make sure you borrow as much as you need from the federal government before looking to private lenders. The government's subsidized and unsubsidized loans offer many benefits, including lower interest rates and, in the case of subsidized loans, deferral of interest until after graduation. Private loan interest rates will be based on your and your student's credit scores as well as overall lending rates. If you are going to take out parent loans from private lenders or the government's Parent PLUS program, make sure you consider your other financial obligations, including your own retirement savings.

As we reviewed in Chapter Six, when your student is off to college, the costs can begin to mount. It is important to prepare a budget together and to know what other expenses you will have in addition to tuition, housing, and food costs.

We understand that this process can be overwhelming and filled with many emotions: anxiety, excitement, frustration, uncertainty, joy, and the list goes on. We hope that this book can be a support to you and your family as you navigate difficult conversations about your finances and your future.

We love hearing college success stories, so please share them with us at betteroff@edmit.me.

Best of luck!

APPENDIX

Using Edmit to be Better Off After College

As you may have noticed on the cover of this book, we introduce ourselves as the cofounders of Edmit. So, what is Edmit?

Edmit (www.edmit.me) is a website that helps you follow the advice in this book. It provides research tools, personalized reports, and an online learning center to help your family every step of the way.

Our guides can provide more detail on the material in this book, starting with how much to save and how to save. We also have more detailed articles on all aspects of the financial aid process—from Q&A articles on how different situations will be treated on the FAFSA, to lists of the most generous colleges for merit- or need-based aid.

When you sign up and set up a profile, Edmit helps you find schools that are a great financial fit and that align with your student's interests: where they want to go geographically, what they want to major in, the size of school, and other factors that might be important to you and them. We have data on the generosity of colleges with respect to need-based and merit-based aid so you can find the colleges that will give you a great price.

In the book, we talk about a rule of thumb that you should only borrow as much as you will earn during your first year after college. This information can be hard to find and calculate, but Edmit makes it easy. You can enter details on how you plan to pay in order to see what gaps you might have, and our software will show you what your total expected debt will be—and warn you if it's a stretch.

During senior year, Edmit helps you evaluate your options and choose the college that will set you up for long-term success. After you get your financial aid letters, you can upload them and we can help you interpret them and determine the best strategy for an appeal. Once you have your final costs, you can use our student loan calculator to evaluate your loan options.

Edmit's software has been designed to be easy to use and understand, but we also offer consultations with our team of college financial counselors. They can help you interpret the information you've collected and talk through the considerations.

It's free to sign up for an Edmit account, and our Edmit Plus membership provides additional features. Readers of this book are eligible for a free month of Edmit Plus—to get your free month, please email us at betteroff@edmit.me

About the Authors

Sabrina Manville and Nick Ducoff are parents and former university administrators committed to helping students and families be better off after college. Their work has been recognized by the U.S. Department of Education, major foundations, and industry leaders.

Sabrina was previously AVP at Southern New Hampshire University, where she led marketing for their College for America program. She has degrees from Yale (BA) and Stanford (MBA). Nick was previously VP at Northeastern University, where he founded one of the first university bootcamp programs. His articles on higher education have been published in the Washington Post, Barron's, CNBC, and Money. He has degrees from Emory (BBA) and the University of Texas at Austin (JD).

In 2017 they co-founded Edmit (www.edmit.me), which provides award-winning tools and advice to families about planning and paying for college.

Made in the USA
Lexington, KY
15 December 2019